While developed using the Burton Stove Top Grill™, many recipes are adaptable for use on outdoor grills or indoor broiling.

LINDA BURTON, MAX BURTON ENTERPRISES, AND THE BURTON STOVE TOP GRILL

The story of Linda Burton, Max Burton Enterprises, and the Burton Stove Top Grill is the continuing story of ingenuity and the capability of a small, family-owned and operated business to succeed and prosper.

Linda Burton's paternal grandfather made quality kitchen items in the "old country" tradition. He believed in the pride of craftsmanship and in the quality of handmade goods. He became the inspiration and the mentor of what was eventually to become Max Burton Enterprises.

In 1976, Max Burton, Linda's father, returned to his earliest roots and the family tradition; he began making hand-forged burner covers on a tiny kiln in his garage.

By 1979, word of Max Burton's fine craftsmanship had spread, his business was growing, and Max Burton Enterprises was born. For the next seven years, the Company produced burner covers and other kitchen accessories.

During a business trip made to the Orient in 1986, Max and Linda discovered an age-old cooking method while dining in a small Korean village restaurant. It consisted of a cone-shaped brass grill called a bulgogi, and it was used at their table to prepare a delicious meal. With its unique design, the fat drained away as the meat cooked, leaving it moist and tender, with no grease. The result was so flavorful that Linda and her father immediately began to formulate a method for adapting the grill to American stoves.

Indoor Grilling

*A collection of recipes developed
for the Burton Stove Top Grills™*

by Barbara Grunes

My thanks to Sandi Bradley, Rob Humrickhouse, and David Marion for their help in making this book possible.

The growing concern about cholesterol and saturated fat made the idea even more valuable and practical. Starting with the basic concept of the bulgogi, they re-designed it and developed a totally new cooking product — the Burton Stove Top Grill. It soon proved to be the perfect answer for those who love grilled foods but share a growing concern about their health and lowered cholesterol consumption and who also appreciate a cooking technique that is quick and simple.

Linda Burton's personal journey to become the president of a small but viable American industry involved some dramatic changes along the way. In 1976 she ventured into the world of sales, representing her father's firm. But on her first day of sales calls she was so overwhelmed by the intensity and intimidation of the buyers that she immediately quit the position. Deciding it couldn't be any tougher than sales, she took up a career in law enforcement, becoming a police officer in Seattle.

In 1987, when her father, Max, passed away, Linda took over the operation of Max Burton Enterprises. It was under Linda's direction that the Burton Stove Top Grill came into production. In 1990, Linda's husband, Bob Denovan, and her brother, Alfred Burton, left their careers and joined the family business.

Linda's mother, Evelyn, runs a kitchen gourmet store that successfully tested the grill and provided valuable customer feedback. "Customers like to know that there is a real person, a real face, behind a company," says Linda. "We have a great deal of personal communication with people who have purchased the Burton Stove Top Grill. They give us constant new cooking ideas and application for use of the grill and many new recipe ideas. Many of our new grill accessories are the result of customer requests or suggestions."

BARBARA GRUNES

Well over two million Americans now cook with Barbara, using her books, which range from grilling techniques (seafood, shellfish, and poultry) to baking, from cooking with convection ovens to both American regional and international cuisines. With over twenty-six cookbooks to her credit, Barbara Grunes has rightfully been dubbed "the queen of cookbooks".

For several years a food columnist for the *Chicago Sun Times*, Grunes is currently a contributor to national and local periodicals. She presently resides in the Chicago area with her husband, a site to which her children often return, to sample her latest recipes and experiments in the kitchen.

Barbara Grunes has successfully tapped her experience as a devoted mother of five and her extensive insight into foods and cooking techniques to provide a practical and simplified approach to cooking, without sacrificing elegance, authenticity, or an appreciation for the unusual. Grunes was trained as an educational psychologist and taught psychology before devoting her creative energies to food. You might say, she has become the psychologist of the kitchen.

CONTENTS

INTRODUCTION

In developing and testing the recipes included in this book, I have become incredibly attached to my Burton Stove Top Grill.

I truly believe that it is a perfect kitchen concept and the Burton Stove Top Grill is itself the state of the art for indoor grilling. The foods that I have prepared, coming hot from the Burton grill, have been universally divine.

Above all else, the use of the Burton Stove Top Grill has been fun and exciting for me. It makes grilling inside a joy. Once you have used your Burton Stove Top Grill, you will never run out of ideas for its use, and I sincerely believe that it will take a permanent place on your stove top.

One of the intentions in writing this cookbook has been to demonstrate the strong health advantage to this alternative to frying. The nature of the Burton Stove Top Grill greatly reduces the fat and grease content of many foods, making them more nutritional and healthy while retaining the magnificent flavor of grilled food.

I have included several recipes in this book which utilize the unique features of the Burton Stove Top Grill. Vegetables have long been a delightful aspect of grilling, but on this grill the flavor and texture of grilled vegetables is enhanced by the fact that the steaming effect of the drip pan keeps them moist and juicy, while the high heat of the grill surface allows quick cooking and the retention of the crunchiness which is so often lost in outdoor grilling or steaming.

I have also included two complete dinner party menus that I believe will be both fun to prepare and a terrific hit with your guests. The Dim Sum brunch is a very different and exciting party meal. The Sukiyaki dinner is another Oriental feast that is simple to prepare and will surely bring the applause of your guests.

When you use your Burton grill, think party, whether you are cooking for family or friends. The appetizers make a splendid accompaniment to an early evening gathering, a cocktail party, or a sports-watching afternoon or evening. Consider arranging a variety of meats and vegetables on trays and encouraging your family or guests to choose and grill their own.

The greatest advantage of the Burton Stove Top Grill is its incredible simplicity, convenience and versatility. Preparation and cooking time are vastly minimized, and clean-up is a dream. After allowing the grill to cool, simply wash both pieces with warm, soapy water and a dish cloth. Both pieces are also dishwasher safe.

USING YOUR BURTON STOVE TOP GRILL

Always fill the reservoir of the drip pan with water to begin and refill as necessary; occasionally pouring in a bit of water on the edge of the drip pan. Do not pour water directly on the grill surface, as it will reduce the heat.

Pre-heating the grill is very important. The grill surface must be very hot.

For Gas Stoves: Light stove and adjust the flame <u>before</u> putting grill in place. Make sure flame does not contact the bottom of the grill surface. Pre-heat on medium-high for approximately 3 minutes. It may be necessary to remove the grate in order for the grill to fit. Do not use high heat with the grate removed.

For Electric Stoves: use the small burner with the Original Grill and the large burner with the Super Grill. Pre-heat on high for approximately 8 minutes.

Once you have seared both sides of a cut of meat, poultry or fish, you can turn the heat on your stove down to medium high or even medium for the remainder of the cooking time. The meat should be very juicy and tender when removed from the grill. Always avoid over-cooking.

Cooking times will definitely vary, depending on the type and thickness of your meat, fish, poultry, vegetables, fruits, etc. While you may use a light coating of vegetable oil, olive oil, or cooking spray on the grill surfaces, it is not really necessary with the no-stick SilverStone coating of the grill surface.

To clean your Burton grill, first allow the grill to cool. Both pieces are dishwater safe, or you may use warm, soapy water. Avoid abrasive cleaning pads which will scratch the non-stick surface. With proper care, your Burton Stove Top Grill will look like new even after many uses.

4

SUGGESTIONS...DO'S AND DON'TS

--- I have suggested flavoring the water of the drip pan in a number of recipes. You may use your own judgement and imagination. Many herbs and spices will work well to give a dish a subtle flavor. You may also add red or white wines, beer or fruit juices to the water.

--- Use the whole grill surface. You are certainly not limited to the non-slotted area of the grill surface. In fact, the moisture rising through the slots greatly enhances the cooking, so feel free to move your foods on the surface frequently during grilling.

--- For thicker cuts of meat, poultry, fish and vegetables, I recommend using the Grill Lid over the surface of the grill. The high heat will sear the food, while the lid will assist in cooking the thicker cuts thoroughly.

--- You can also use your Burton Grill directly at tableside, grilling with a "Mr. Max" portable burner. The theatrics are terrific, and the food will be both elegant and savory.

--- I do recommend and have included in many recipes, the use of marinade. Marinading most dishes will add flavor and serve to tenderize the food.

---   I often use a small amount of Burton Mesquite Liquid Smoke in the water as a subtle taste addition. It can also be sprinkled directly on meats as they grill for an authentic outdoor flavor.

---   For kabobs, I strongly recommend the use of wooden skewers. Wooden skewers should be soaked in water before use on the grill.

---   Almost all recipes or favorite dishes which you have prepared on your outside grill can easily be adapted to the Burton Stove Top Grill, and rain, snow and cold will no longer limit your ability to enjoy grilled meals.

---   Do not use metal utensils, such as a metal spatula, on the grill surface. Use plastic or wooden kitchen utensils.

APPETIZERS

Appetizers serve to excite the appetite and to prepare the palate for the ensuing courses of a meal. They have a very historic and significant function in culinary history. As finger food or hors d'oeuvres, they heighten a feeling of camaraderie and are an attractive and scrumptious addition to entertaining.

We feel that appetizers are too often a "company-only" type of cooking. In fact, the occasional addition of a hot appetizer will not only spice up a routine family meal, but it will also serve as a delightful taste complement or contrast to the evening entrée.

Whether you are preparing for a formal dinner party, a cocktail party, or merely adding zest to a family dinner, the Burton grill is perfectly designed for producing "sure-hit" hot appetizers.

This chapter includes a wide variety of recipes from a Dim Sum Brunch, to Maryland Crab Cakes with Tartar Sauce, to Miniature Burgers on Whole Wheat Rolls.

DIM SUM BRUNCH

Makes 8 to 10 servings

Stuffed Shiitake Mushrooms
Stuffed Sweet Peppers
Noodles with Chinese Barbecued Pork
Rumaki Brushed with Pineapple Sauce
Gingered Papaya

Many of these recipes can easily be prepared before and frozen until just before serving time. The barbecued pork, stuffed mushrooms and stuffed peppers can all be prepared, frozen and reheated at serving time. For complete authentic atmosphere, use chopsticks.

Dim Sum means "something to dot the heart with". The concept of serving a group of many small dishes began in the tea houses of Canton. This wonderful array of dishes is usually served around lunch time.

Ingredients, including sesame oil, chili paste, shiitake mushrooms, snow peas and Chinese five spice powder can be purchased at many supermarkets.

Shiitake is the Japanese name for a mushroom that can be found either fresh or dried in most Oriental food stores or large supermarkets. The taste of the Shiitake is full-bodied and heady. The dried shiitakes, which are used in the following recipe, must be reconstituted by soaking them in water.

STUFFED SHIITAKE MUSHROOMS

Makes 8 to 10 servings

18 to 20 large dried mushrooms, washed, with stems removed
1/2 cup dry sherry

Filling

1/4 pound lean pork, cut in 3/4 inch cubes
1/4 pound uncooked shrimp, washed, deveined, patted dry
6 water chestnuts
1 egg white
1 tablespoon cornstarch

Peanut oil for brushing grill

Sauce

3 green onions, minced
6 tablespoons soy sauce
2 tablespoons dry sherry

Stuffed Shiitake Mushrooms

Cover mushrooms with hot water in a large bowl. Mix in sherry. Soak mushrooms for 1 hour at room temperature. Drain and squeeze mushrooms dry. Set aside.

Chop pork, shrimp and water chestnuts with egg white and cornstarch in food processor fitted with steel blade.

Stuff mushroom caps with pork mixture.

To make sauce, mix onions, soy sauce and sherry in small saucepan. Cook sauce over medium heat, until warm, stirring often. Remove from heat.

Preheat Burton Stove Top Grill. Brush grill surface lightly with oil.

Cook stuffed mushrooms, meat side down, over medium heat approximately 2 minutes. Turn mushrooms over and grill about 1 minute. Meat should be moist, yet crusty. Remove to serving dish and drizzle with sauce. Serve hot.

Use large, red sweet bell peppers. Cut the peppers in quarters lengthwise. Stuff peppers with Oriental stuffing and cook on the grill with the meat side down to make the stuffing crusty.

STUFFED SWEET PEPPERS

Makes 12 stuffed pepper pieces

Filling

6 ounces ground pork
1 green onion, minced
1/2 teaspoon powdered ginger
2 tablespoons water chestnuts, minced
2 tablespoons dry sherry
1 1/2 tablespoons soy sauce
1/4 teaspoon salt

3 red or green bell peppers, seeded and quartered lengthwise.
  Cut along ridges to form natural containers
4 tablespoons cornstarch

Peanut oil for brushing grill

Sauce

3 tablespoons soy sauce
1/2 cup water
1 teaspoon sugar

Stuffed Sweet Peppers

Mix together pork, onion, ginger, water chestnuts, sherry, soy sauce and salt in a bowl. Set aside. For easy preparation, these ingredients can be minced together in a food processor fitted with a steel blade.

Stuff pepper pieces with pork mixture. Spread cornstarch in a flat dish and press stuffed side into cornstarch. Tap off excess cornstarch. Place on dish and set aside.

Prepare sauce by combining soy sauce, water and sugar in a small saucepan. Cook over medium heat until sauce is heated, about 3 minutes. Reserve.

Preheat Burton Stove Top Grill. Brush grill surface lightly with oil. Grill stuffed sweet peppers, stuffed side down for 1 to 2 minutes, or until stuffing is cooked on the inside and crisp on the outside. Turn peppers over and grill about 1 minute to cook pepper.

Remove stuffed peppers to serving dish and drizzle with sauce.

Serve hot.

NOODLES WITH CHINESE BARBECUED PORK

Makes 5 to 6 servings

14 ounces soft noodles, or pasta, cooked according
    to package directions
5 green onions, minced
1/2 pound fresh bean sprouts, washed with hot water,
    drained
1/2 pound heated barbecued pork slices (recipe follows)
1 cup snow peas, trimmed

Sauce

5 tablespoons soy sauce
1 teaspoon dark brown sugar
1/2 teaspoon salt
2 tablespoons dry sherry
1 teaspoon sesame oil

Place cooked noodles in deep bowl. Cut noodles with kitchen scissors into 3 inch pieces. Mix in onions, bean sprouts, pork and snow peas.

To prepare sauce, mix together soy sauce, sugar, salt, sherry and sesame oil. Toss noodles with sauce. Serve hot or room temperature.

The word Hoi-sin in Chinese means literally, "sea-freshness sauce". While poetic in meaning, this sauce is actually wheat or soybean based.

The barbecued pork can be used as an appetizer or main dish. This recipe freezes well. Make it ahead of time and defrost as needed.

CHINESE BARBECUE PORK

Makes 3 servings

1 pound boneless pork loin, partially frozen, then sliced into thin strips

Five Spice Marinade

2 tablespoons sugar
1/4 teaspoon salt
2 cloves garlic, minced
1 teaspoon five-spice powder
1/4 cup soy sauce
1/4 cup Hoi-sin sauce
1/4 cup sake or dry white wine

Peanut oil for brushing grill

Topping

1 tablespoon soy sauce
4 tablespoons honey
1/2 teaspoon sesame oil

Chinese Barbecue Pork

To prepare marinade, combine sugar, salt, garlic, five spice powder, soy sauce, Hoi-sin sauce and sake in a small bowl. Then pour the marinade into a large self-sealing plastic bag. Add pork strips, seal the bag securely and turn it several times to coat the pork. Refrigerate and marinate for 4 to 6 hours, turning occasionally. Drain pork, discard marinade.

Combine topping ingredients in a small bowl.

Preheat Burton Stove Top Grill. Brush grill surface lightly with oil.

Cook pork in a single layer over high heat, turning as it cooks. Grill approximately 2 to 3 minutes. Pork should be cooked through, but not overcooked. Remove pork to plate. Cool pork. Spoon barbecued pork into plastic bags, seal and freeze until needed.

This sauce is a combination of pineapple and soy sauce and makes a classic recipe adapted for use with the Burton Grill.

RUMAKI BRUSHED WITH PINEAPPLE SAUCE

Makes 8 servings

Pineapple Brushing Sauce

1/2 cup sugar
1/2 cup cider vinegar
2 teaspoons soy sauce
1/4 cup pineapple juice
4 tablespoons catsup

8 chicken livers, cut in half, discard gristle
8 water chestnuts, drained, cut in half
4 slices lean bacon, cut in half

8 small bamboo skewers or toothpicks, soaked in water 10 minutes, drained

To prepare sauce, combine sugar, vinegar, soy sauce, pineapple juice and catsup in small saucepan. Bring mixture to a boil over medium heat. Reduce heat to simmer and continue cooking 3 minutes, stirring often. Cool sauce.

Rumaki Brushed With Pineapple Sauce

Arrange each liver half on top of a water chestnut piece. Wrap a strip of bacon around the liver and chestnut. Skewer with a toothpick or a bamboo skewer. Brush rumaki with pineapple brushing sauce.

Preheat Burton Stove Top Grill. Cook rumaki over medium-high heat until liver is cooked and bacon crisp, turning 2 or 3 times. Brush rumaki with sauce as you turn. Remove rumaki from grill and set decoratively on serving dish. Good with grilled green onion strips. Have guests help themselves.

Ginger is actually a root with a highly aromatic fragrance and a sharp and pungent flavor. Fresh ginger, which can now be found in most supermarkets, is a mainstay of Chinese cooking. Fresh ginger should be rock-hard with a smooth, tannish skin.

To grate, the root should first be peeled. Then grate on a fine grater. I use a ceramic grater purchased in an Oriental food store. It is inexpensive and works well. Ginger should be stored in a cool, dry place.

GINGERED PAPAYA

Makes 8 servings

3 papayas, ripe but firm
2 teaspoons grated fresh ginger
1/8 teaspoon grated nutmeg
2 tablespoons freshly squeezed lime juice
1/4 cup butter or margarine, melted
3 lettuce leaves
1 lime, sliced thinly for garnish

Peel, seed and slice papayas into 1/2 inch pieces.

Mix ginger, nutmeg and lime juice into the melted butter. Brush papaya slices with butter mixture.

Gingered Papaya

Preheat Burton Stove Top Grill. Cook papaya over medium heat, for 30 to 45 seconds on each side. Papaya will be warm but still firm. Brush with melted butter as you turn papaya.

To serve, arrange warm papaya slices on lettuce leaves and garnish with lime slices.

Lump crab meat, used in this recipe, can be either fresh or frozen. However, fresh crab will have a sweeter and more savory taste.

MARYLAND CRAB CAKES

Makes 4 servings, 1 crab cake per person

Tartar Sauce (recipe follows)

6 ounces lump crabmeat, fresh or frozen (defrosted)
1 tablespoon minced parsley
1/4 cup mayonnaise
1/4 teaspoon each ingredient: salt, white pepper
1/2 teaspoon each ingredient: dry mustard, Worcestershire sauce
1 cup fine bread crumbs

Butter or margarine to brush grill

Pick over the crab meat, discarding any gristle.

Mix together crabmeat, parsley, mayonnaise, salt, pepper, mustard, and Worcestershire sauce in a bowl. Form into crab cakes.

Spread the bread crumbs on a flat dish. Lightly bread the crab cakes. Set crab cakes on a dish and refrigerate before cooking.

Maryland Crab Cakes

Preheat Burton Stove Top Grill. Brush grill surface with melted butter. Grill crab cakes over medium heat, turning once during grilling.

Crab cakes will be lightly browned on the outside and cooked on the inside. Remove crab cakes from the grill and place 1 cake on each dish. Good with tartar sauce and garlic flavored mayonnaise mixed with low-fat, plain yogurt. Recipe can easily be doubled if you are expecting more guests.

Tartar Sauce

Makes 1 1/4 cup sauce

1 cup mayonnaise
1 small red onion, minced
1 1/2 tablespoon each ingredient: chopped sweet pickles, drained capers

Blend together mayonnaise, onion, pickle and capers in a bowl. Cover and refrigerate sauce until ready to serve. Stir sauce before serving.

When slicing meat for kabobs, strips or Oriental dishes, the meat should be partially frozen before slicing. Then slice meat across the grain.

SKEWERED STEAK STRIPS WITH
OYSTER/GARLIC BRUSHING SAUCE

Makes 24 pieces, serve 2 to 3 per person

Oyster/Garlic Brushing Sauce

2 green onions, minced
1/4 cup soy sauce
1/4 cup chicken stock
1/4 cup dark brown sugar, firmly packed
1 teaspoon powdered ginger
2 cloves garlic, minced
3 tablespoons oyster sauce, available at Oriental food stores
1 1/2 tablespoons dark molasses
1 tablespoon dry white wine
1 tablespoon cornstarch blended with 1 tablespoon cold water

1 pound flank steak
24 8-inch skewers, soaked in water 10 minutes, drained
Kiwi fruit slices, garnish

To prepare sauce, heat all sauce ingredients, except cornstarch mixture, in a saucepan. Heat sauce to a boil over medium heat. Stir often. Reduce mixture to simmer. Continue cooking until ingredients are well blended, about 3 minutes. Stir in cornstarch mixture, stir and cook until sauce thickens slightly. Cool.

Skewered Steak Strips with Oyster/Garlic Brushing Sauce

Slice partially frozen meat diagonally, across the grain, into 1 inch strips. Thread meat onto skewers, in and out until the meat is securely on the skewer. Brush skewered steak with sauce.

Preheat Burton Stove Top Grill. Grill skewered steak over medium-high heat, turning as needed to cook steak. Brush meat with sauce as you turn it. Meat will be cooked to taste, and browned on the outside. Remove meat from grill. Skewered steak can be kept warm in a 250 degree F oven. Serve hot. Good with extra sauce for dipping. Garnish with kiwi fruit slices.

Figs are small, luscious fruits bursting with a soft, sweet flavor. Fresh figs are available in the fall in many produce departments. If fresh figs are unavailable, dried figs may be used, but they must first be reconstituted by soaking them in warm water for twenty minutes. Serve this recipe with sherry and either grapes or a mixed green salad. This recipe works well as either an appetizer or as a tasty lunch.

CHICKEN LIVERS WITH GRILLED FRESH FIGS

Makes 8 servings

1 1/2 pounds chicken livers
3 tablespoons butter or margarine
1/2 teaspoon dried sage
1/4 teaspoon each ingredient: salt, pepper, dried oregano
1/4 small onion, sliced
2 teaspoons dry sherry
3 tablespoons minced parsley

Cut chicken livers in half, discard gristle.

Melt butter; stir in sage, salt, pepper and dried oregano. Set aside.

Preheat Burton Stove Top Grill. Cook onions and liver over medium heat about 1 to 2 minutes, or until livers are browned, but still slightly pink inside. Do not overcook livers. Brush with melted seasoned butter as they grill. Place cooked livers in serving bowl. Sprinkle with sherry and parsley. Serve with toothpicks, whole wheat triangles and grilled figs (recipe follows).

GRILLED FIGS

Makes 8 servings

8 ripe fresh figs
2 tablespoons butter or margarine, melted
2 tablespoons light brown sugar

Slice the figs in half; brush cut side with butter and sprinkle with sugar.

Preheat Burton Stove Top Grill. Brush grill surface with butter. Grill figs cut side down until golden brown, about 1 1/2 minutes over medium heat. Watch that the sugar doesn't brown. Grill until sugar melts and figs are warm.

Remove the figs from the grill and place cut side up around the livers.

These are an especially popular and appropriate item for children's parties or football watching parties.

For best results, grind your own beef or choose your meat and ask the butcher to grind it for you.

MINIATURE BURGERS ON WHOLE WHEAT ROLLS

Makes 8 servings

Whole Wheat Rolls (recipe follows)

2 pounds ground chuck steak
1 onion, minced
1 teaspoon Worcestershire sauce
1/2 teaspoon each ingredient: salt, garlic powder, dry mustard
1/4 teaspoon pepper
1 egg (or 2 egg whites)

Extra virgin olive oil for brushing grill

Combine ground meat, onion, Worcestershire sauce, salt, garlic powder, mustard, pepper and egg. Shape meat into 16 miniature hamburger patties. Set patties on dish and refrigerate until grilling time.

Miniature Burgers On Whole Wheat Rolls

Preheat Burton Stove Top Grill. Brush grill surface lightly with oil. Grill hamburger patties over high heat. Burgers will be crusty on the outside and cooked to taste on the inside. Turn once or twice during cooking. Remove burgers and place on warm whole wheat roll.

Serve burgers with chips, pickles, lettuce, tomato slices, relish, mustard and catsup.

Yeasts are living organisms which feed on sugars and produce alcohol and carbon dioxide, which causes the "rising" that we desire. Yeast is very dependent on definite temperature ranges. It activates best between 78 degrees and 82 degrees, although dry yeast needs to be dissolved in water heated between 105 degrees and 115 degrees. Either dry or compressed yeast is satisfactory, although dry yeast is preferred by many as it keeps much better than compressed yeast.

WHOLE WHEAT HAMBURGER ROLLS
WITH POPPY SEEDS

Makes 16 Miniature Rolls

1 package active dry yeast
3/4 cup warm water, between 105 and 110 degrees F
1 teaspoon sugar
2 to 2 1/2 cups unbleached all-purpose flour
1/2 cup whole wheat flour
2 1/2 tablespoons butter or margarine, melted, cooled
1/2 teaspoon salt
1 egg white, slightly beaten
1/2 cup poppy seeds

Fit dough hook into electric mixer.

Sprinkle yeast over water mixed with sugar in the electric mixer bowl. Let stand in a draft free area until yeast foams, about 5 minutes.

Whole Wheat Hamburger Rolls With Poppy Seeds

Mix in 1 cup of all-purpose flour and the whole wheat flour. Add butter and salt. Blend until a soft dough is formed, adding more of the all-purpose flour as needed.

Divide dough into 16 equal pieces; shape into hamburger rolls and set on non-stick cookie sheet. Cover lightly with towel and place in a draft free area for 35 to 40 minutes. Dough will double in bulk.

Push down on buns with your hand. Cover and again let dough rise in draft free area, about 25 to 30 minutes.

Brush top of rolls with egg white and sprinkle with poppy seeds.

Preheat oven to 350 degrees F. Bake rolls for 25 minutes. The rolls are done when the top of the rolls are a golden brown. Cool rolls on a wire rack. Slice and serve warm.

ENGLISH MUFFIN PIZZAS

Makes 6 servings

Extra virgin olive oil for brushing grill
3 split English muffins
6 thin slices Mozzarella cheese (English muffin size)
6 tablespoons tomato paste or catsup
Oregano, garlic powder, pepper or red pepper flakes, to taste

Preheat Burton Stove Top Grill. Brush grill surface lightly with olive oil. Cook English muffins, cut side down, pressing down with a spatula, over medium-high heat, about 1 minute. Turn English muffin over. Place a slice of cheese on top of muffin. Grill about 1 minute. The muffin will have golden brown areas on top and on the bottom. The cheese will warm and begin to melt along the edges.

Remove muffins from the grill and set on a dish. Place 1 tablespoon of tomato sauce on the center of each muffin. Spread sauce to cover most of top of the muffin using the back of a teaspoon. Sprinkle muffin with oregano, garlic powder and pepper to taste.

Serve muffins hot. Be creative and add toppings that you may enjoy, such as chopped green bell pepper, sliced mushrooms, anchovy strips or chopped onion. Or you may have small bowls of the toppings and let your guests sprinkle their own toppings over the muffin pizzas.

BREAKFAST ENGLISH MUFFIN WITH CANADIAN BACON

Makes 6 servings

Extra virgin olive oil for brushing grill
3 split English muffins
6 slices Canadian bacon or Canadian style bacon
1 tomato, cut into 6 thin slices
1 onion, cut into 6 thin rounds of onion
Dried basil to taste

Preheat Burton Stove Top Grill. Brush grill surface lightly with olive oil. Cook English muffins, cut side down, pressing down with a spatula over medium-high heat. Grill about 1 minute. Turn English muffin over. Grill 1 minute longer or until golden brown on bottom. The muffin will be golden brown on top also. Remove muffins to serving plate. Grill bacon, about 1 minute on each side or until cooked to taste. Layer a bacon strip on each muffin.

Set a tomato slice over bacon. Grill onion about 30 seconds on each side. Onion will char slightly. Place onion or onion rings on top of tomato. Sprinkle with basil. Serve immediately.

Chinese ingredients are available at large supermarkets or in Oriental food stores.

BEEF ROLL AROUNDS

Makes 6 servings

Honey Brushing Sauce

3 tablespoons soy sauce
2 tablespoons honey
2 tablespoons dry white wine
2 tablespoons oyster sauce
1/4 teaspoon each ingredient: powdered garlic, Chinese five-
    spice powder
3 stalks celery
1/2 pound beef tenderloin

To prepare honey brushing sauce, mix the sauce ingredients together in a bowl. Set aside.

Chill meat. Cut into 18 thin slices. Press meat slices with a spatula.

Cut celery stalks in half horizontally. Then cut celery again into 3 inch pieces, making 18 3-inch stalks. Roll a piece of meat around each celery stalk, cigarette style. Brush beef roll arounds with sauce.

Beef Roll Arounds

Preheat Burton Stove Top Grill. Grill beef roll arounds, seam side down, over medium-high heat. Turn roll arounds as they cook, brushing with sauce as you turn. Meat is done when pinkness is gone.

Remove appetizers to serving dish. Serve hot. Good with cooked oriental noodles or fried rice.

GRILLED SHRIMP SUSHI

Makes 6 servings

1/2 pound short grain rice, washed, drained well
1 tablespoon dry white wine
2 tablespoons rice vinegar
2 teaspoons sugar
1/2 teaspoon salt
12 extra large shrimp, deveined, butterflied, washed,
**   flattened, patted dry**
2 teaspoons lightly toasted sesame seeds
Pickled ginger

Put rice in saucepan, cover with water.

Bring mixture to a boil, reduce heat to simmer, cover and continue cooking for 15 minutes.

Meanwhile, heat vinegar, sugar and salt in small pan. Bring to a boil. Remove from heat, cool.

When rice is finished cooking, remove from heat and let cool for 15 minutes. Spoon rice into a bowl. Sprinkle rice with vinegar mixture, mix well.

Form rice into oval patties, the size of the shrimp, and set on a platter.

Grilled Shrimp Sushi

Preheat Burton Stove Top Grill. Over medium-high heat grill shrimp, cut side down. Turn shrimp over and grill only until done. Do not overcook shrimp. Shrimp is done when it turns opaque.

To assemble, place a shrimp over each rice patty and sprinkle with sesame seeds. Serve with pickled ginger at room temperature.

These succulent and spicy appetizers are prepared using chili paste with garlic, which is available in Oriental food stores.

CHILI SEA SCALLOP KABOBS

Makes 6 servings

Chili Brushing Sauce

2 tablespoons peanut oil
1 medium onion, minced
1/2 teaspoon each ingredient: powdered ginger, minced garlic, red pepper flakes
1/4 cup soy sauce
3 tablespoons light brown sugar
3 tablespoons chili paste with garlic, available at Oriental food stores, or substitute catsup
3 tablespoons red wine vinegar

12 sea scallops
24 snow peas, trimmed
12 8-inch bamboo skewers, soaked in water 10 minutes, drained

Sea Scallop Kabobs

To prepare sauce, heat 2 tablespoons of the peanut oil in a pan. Sauté onion with ginger, garlic and red pepper flakes for 2 minutes, stirring often. Add remaining sauce ingredients. Simmer 1 minute to combine ingredients.

Thread scallops and snow peas alternately onto skewers. Brush with sauce.

Preheat Burton Stove Top Grill. Grill kabobs over medium heat, turning once or twice during grilling or as needed. Kabobs should be cooked through, but not overcooked. Scallops become firm and opaque. Remove kabobs from grill and serve one to a guest. Good with hot white rice or fried rice.

Szechuan is a province in central China. This province is the home of pandas and hot peppers. The cuisine of Szechuan is fast becoming one of the most popular Chinese foods in the Western world.

SZECHUAN CHICKEN WINGS

Makes 8 servings

Szechuan Brushing Sauce

1/2 cup soy sauce
3 tablespoons apricot jam
1/4 cup dry white wine
2 green onions, minced
1/2 teaspoon grated ginger
2 cloves garlic, minced
1/3 cup firmly packed dark brown sugar
2 teaspoons chili paste with garlic, available at Oriental food
    stores
1/8 teaspoon red pepper flakes

16 green onions, trimmed

2 pounds chicken wings
Peanut oil for brushing grill and green onions

Szechuan Chicken Wings

To prepare Szechuan brushing sauce, combine soy sauce, jam, wine, onions, ginger, garlic, sugar, chili paste and red pepper flakes in a bowl. Set aside.

Remove tips from chicken wings. Cut wings in half at joint. Wash wings and pat dry. Brush wing pieces with Szechuan brushing sauce.

Preheat Burton Stove Top Grill. Brush grill surface lightly with peanut oil and cook wing pieces at medium-high heat until grilled. Wings will brown on the outside and be cooked on the inside. Juices will run clear when thickest area of wings are cut with a knife and meat becomes opaque. Turn wings several times during grilling and brush wings with sauce as you turn. Remove wings to serving platter. Serve hot.

Brush green onions lightly with peanut oil. Cook onions on preheated grill over medium-high heat. Turn onions once during grilling, cook about 1 minute on each side. Serve onions hot with chicken wings.

Anchovies are small, silvery fish which are best known as canned fillets packed in oil. Anchovies have a distinctive, highly salty flavor, and they are widely used as a garnish to other foods.

ANCHOVY TOAST

Makes 8 servings

16 thin slices of day old white bread, crust removed
2 cans, 2 ounces each, anchovy fillets, drained
16 thin slices of Mozzarella cheese
1/2 teaspoon each ingredient: garlic powder, dried basil
Butter or margarine for brushing grill

Cut each slice of bread in half. Place 1 slice of cheese on each of 16 pieces. Set 2 anchovy filets on the top of cheese and sprinkle with small amount of garlic and basil. Make a sandwich, covering the anchovy side of bread with remaining bread, pressing the sandwich together.

Preheat Burton Stove Top Grill. Brush grill surface with butter. Cook sandwiches over medium-high heat until golden brown, about 1 minute per side. Turn carefully, and grill other side of sandwich until golden brown. Press sandwich together gently with spatula. Remove anchovy toast to plate. Serve hot. Good with antipasto or tossed salad or tomato wedges.

This is a quickly prepared recipe which is perfect for spontaneous company. Pineapple, salami and red peppers make an interesting and savory combination of tastes.

SALAMI/PINEAPPLE KABOBS

Makes 6 servings (12 small kabobs)

Brown Sugar Brushing Sauce

4 tablespoons soy sauce
2 1/2 tablespoons dark brown sugar
2 tablespoons red wine vinegar

24 pieces pineapple chunks, drained
24 1/2-inch chunks of salami
12 strips red or green bell pepper

12 small bamboo skewers or toothpicks, soaked in water 10 minutes, drained

To make brown sugar brushing sauce, combine soy sauce, sugar and vinegar in a bowl. If you like, you can substitute a bottled chutney for brushing sauce.

Thread a pineapple chunk, a piece of salami and repeat a pineapple chunk, pieces of salami, and a strip of pepper alternately on each skewer. Brush with sauce or chutney.

Salami/Pineapple Kabobs

Preheat Burton Stove Top Grill. Cook kabobs over medium-high heat until done to taste. Turn kabobs 2 to 3 times and brush with sauce as you turn. Salami will brown slightly. Remove kabobs to serving dish. Serve hot.

Saté is an Indonesian appetizer in which cubes of meat are skewered and grilled.

PORK SATÉ WITH GINGER MARINADE

Makes 24 saté about 8 to 10 servings

Ginger Marinade

4 green onions, minced
2 1/2 teaspoons freshly grated ginger root
2 cloves garlic, minced
3 tablespoons freshly squeezed lime juice
1/2 teaspoon salt
1/4 teaspoon each ingredient: red pepper flakes, or to taste,
    ground cumin
4 tablespoons water
2 pounds pork tenderloin, sliced about 3/4 inch thick, cut into
    1/2 inch pieces
24 8-inch bamboo skewers, soaked in water 10 minutes,
    drained

Chunky Peanut Sauce

2 tablespoons peanut oil
3 green onions, minced
2 cloves garlic, minced
1/8 teaspoon red pepper flakes, or to taste
1 3/4 cups strong chicken stock
3/4 cup roughly chopped peanuts (use food processor fitted
    with steel blade)

Pork Saté With Ginger Marinade

1 tablespoon freshly squeezed lime juice
2 tablespoons dark brown sugar
2 tablespoons minced cilantro, or to taste

Makes 1 1/2 cups

Combine marinade ingredients and pour the marinade into a large self-sealing plastic bag. Add meat and seal the bag securely closed and turn it several times to coat the meat. Refrigerate and marinate for 2 to 3 hours, turning occasionally. Drain the meat, discard marinade.

Meanwhile, prepare chunky peanut sauce. Heat oil in saucepan. Sauté onions, garlic and red pepper flakes for 2 minutes, stir often. Mix in stock, peanuts, juice, sugar and cilantro. Simmer for 5 to 6 minutes, stir often. Serve sauce hot. Set aside until serving time. If sauce thickens, just add hot water, 2 tablespoons at a time, until desired thickness.

Thread pork chunks onto skewers. Preheat Burton Stove Top Grill. Grill saté over medium-high heat until pork is cooked, slightly charred on the outside and all traces of pink are gone. Turn often grilling all sides of pork. Remove sate from grill and arrange on a serving dish. Serve saté hot with chunky peanut sauce.

Rosemary is a very pungent herb. I grow rosemary in a pot in my kitchen all year around. It grows and grows, and I clip it off when I need it. Rosemary is handsome and makes a pretty centerpiece or garnish as well as a flavoring for meats and wild game. Sprinkle rosemary on the water in the grill for extra flavoring.

ROSEMARY LAMB RIBS

Makes 4 to 5 servings

Rosemary Marinade

1 teaspoon dried rosemary
1/2 teaspoon each ingredient: salt, freshly ground black
     pepper
1 1/2 cups catsup
3 cloves garlic, minced
1 small onion, minced
3/4 cup grape jelly, melted with 2 tablespoons water
1 teaspoon Worcestershire sauce
1 tablespoon red wine vinegar

2 tablespoons dried rosemary
3 1/2 to 4 pounds lamb ribs, remove all visible fat

Combine rosemary marinade ingredients.

Rosemary Lamb Ribs

Cut ribs into 2 rib sections. Pour marinade into 2 large self-sealing plastic bags. Divide ribs between the two bags and seal closed. Turn bags several times to coat the meat. Refrigerate and marinate for 3 to 4 hours, turning occasionally. Drain the meat, reserve marinade.

Preheat Burton Stove Top Grill. Sprinkle dried rosemary in the water pan. Replace grill surface. Grill ribs over medium-high heat, turning as needed. Ribs should be crisp on the outside and cooked on the inside. Brush with marinade as you turn ribs.

Remove ribs from the grill. Serve ribs hot. Good with Greek salad and eggplant relish (recipe follows).

This spicy relish is excellent spread on white-flour crackers (thin, flour wafers). Eggplant relish is also superb with fresh-cut vegetables.

EGGPLANT RELISH

Makes 4 to 6 servings

1 eggplant, washed, peeled, trim off end, cut into 1/2 inch slices
3 tablespoons extra virgin olive oil
1 onion, minced
5 stalks celery, chopped
1 cup mushrooms, chopped
1 large tomato, chopped
2 tablespoons freshly squeezed lemon juice
1/3 cup tomato juice
3 tablespoons catsup
3/4 teaspoon each ingredient: dried oregano, dried basil
1/2 teaspoon each ingredient: salt, fresh ground black pepper

Brush eggplant slices lightly with olive oil.

Preheat Burton Stove Top Grill. Cook eggplant over medium-high heat until tender. Eggplant will brown on the outside and be tender on the inside. Remove eggplant from grill and mash in a bowl.

Eggplant Relish

Stir in remaining ingredients and mix well. Taste to adjust seasonings.

Cover eggplant relish and refrigerate until serving time. Stir before serving. Good with sesame crackers and cut vegetables.

CHEESE FINGERS

Makes 8 servings

1 pound low-fat mozzarella cheese
2 eggs, lightly beaten
1/4 teaspoon each ingredient: salt, pepper, dried basil
3/4 cup all-purpose flour
1 1/2 cups fine white breadcrumbs

Cut cheese in 3 inch long and 1/2 inch thick fingers. Season beaten eggs with salt, pepper and basil. Roll cheese fingers in bread crumbs. Coat with egg and roll in bread crumbs once again.

Preheat Burton Stove Top Grill. Grill cheese fingers over medium heat, about 30 seconds on each side, until coating is lightly browned. Serve hot with cut vegetables and garlic bread.

This recipe can very effectively be prepared ahead and frozen.

CHEESE COINS

Makes 3 dozen

1/2 pound cheddar cheese, shredded
3 tablespoons butter or margarine, room temperature
3/4 cup unbleached all-purpose flour
1/2 teaspoon cumin seeds
1 teaspoon Worcestershire sauce
1/4 teaspoon each ingredient: salt, white pepper

Place all ingredients into a food processor fitted with steel blade. Process about 40 seconds or until all ingredients are combined.

Shape batter into 2 logs about 1 1/2 inches thick. Wrap securely in wax paper. Chill cheese logs until firm.

At serving time, slice cheese logs into 1/4 inch rounds.

Preheat Burton Stove Top Grill. Cook cheese rounds over medium heat only until warm, turn once with a spatula, about 30 seconds each side. Serve immediately. Good served with dark bread slices and Greek olives.

I discovered my daughter, Dorothy, and two friends making gyros on my Burton Grill. They cooked the lamb mixture and then warmed pita bread sheets on the grill. For gyro appetizers, cut pita bread gyros into quarters and serve with cucumber dressing.

DOROTHY'S GYROS PITA POCKETS WITH YOGURT CUCUMBER DRESSING

Makes 6 servings

1 1/2 cups low-fat, plain yogurt
1/2 cup finely chopped cucumber
1/4 teaspoon each ingredient: garlic powder, salt, white pepper

18 (or more to taste) slices of Gyros meat, available at supermarkets
6 whole wheat or plain pita bread rounds, cut in half, open pockets
1 large red onion, chopped
1 large tomato, chopped

To make cucumber dressing, mix together yogurt, cucumber, garlic, salt and pepper in a small bowl. Cover dip and refrigerate until serving time.

Dorothy's Gyros' Pita Pockets With Yogurt Cucumber Dressing

Preheat Burton Stove Top Grill. Grill Gyros' slices a few seconds on each side over high heat or until done to taste. Meat will brown. Remove from grill and blot off excess fat with paper toweling. Grill pita pockets a few seconds on each side until warm. Open pocket and fill with meat and cucumber dressing. Cut each pocket in half, arrange on serving dish. Serve with a bowl of chopped red onion and chopped tomatoes.

SALADS

While salads are not generally connotated with grilling, these recipes make a splendid addition to your repertoire. Salads are traditionally perceived as an addendum to a meal, but I like to think of salad as an overture to the symphony. On the other hand, the salad may very effectively make a refreshing meal in itself, healthy, wholesome, light and totally satisfying. Whatever your desire, the Burton grill will help to simplify your salad preparations, making them fast, easy and delightful.

If the salad dish is to precede the meal, it should be either complementary to the meal itself, or it should serve to pique the palate rather than to fill the stomach, as is far too often the case.

I have designed these salad recipes for use with the Burton grill, combining hot and cold; think of this as a new concept for grilling indoors. The appetites of your family and your guests will be quickened and satisfied by the salads you present to them. Grilling and salad---unique, fun, and now, memorable.

Salads make an ideal solution to many left-over dishes. Both meat and vegetables may be refreshened on the Burton grill and provide the foundation for a terrific salad.

Enjoy a range of recipes from Grilled Pepper Salad, to Seafood Spinach Pasta Salad, to Southwest Chicken Salad.

GRILLED CHICKEN WITH
PECAN AND ORANGE

Makes 4 servings

Dressing

3/4 cup low-fat, plain yogurt
3/4 cup mayonnaise
1/3 cup freshly squeezed orange juice
1 teaspoon orange zest

1 cup chopped pecans
1 pound fettuccine
2 chicken breasts, skinned, boned, cut into 1 inch strips
1/2 teaspoon garlic powder
1 tablespoon extra virgin olive oil
1 can mandarin oranges, drained

To make dressing, combine yogurt, mayonnaise, juice and zest in bowl. Cover and refrigerate until needed.

Spread pecans on a cookie sheet and toast in 350 degree F oven for about 5 to 8 minutes, stirring once. Remove nuts from oven.

Cook fettuccine in boiling water until tender or "al dente", or cook according to package directions, drain. Place in large bowl.

Grilled Chicken With Pecan And Orange Dressing

Preheat Burton Stove Top Grill. Mix garlic powder with oil. Brush chicken with oil and grill over medium-high heat until cooked, turning as needed and cooking 4 to 5 minutes. Chicken will be slightly firm to touch, but don't overcook. Remove chicken from grill. Cut into 1/2 inch cubes.

To serve, toss fettuccine and dressing. Mix in orange segments. Divide onto 4 or 5 salad plates. Place chicken and pecans on top of each salad. Serve warm or cold.

Serve with grilled red onion slices.

Capers are the buds of a bush native to Asia and the Mediterranean. They are pickled in vinegar brine, and they add a sour, pungent taste to this and other chicken, meat and game dishes. Capers will retain their vitality as long as they remain covered by the pickling liquid in the bottle.

The strong taste of Parmesan cheese and the sharp flavor of capers give this chicken salad an interesting and refreshing quality.

Use high quality parmesan cheese and grate it yourself for best results.

ITALIAN CHICKEN SALAD

Makes 4 to 5 servings

1/4 cup extra virgin olive oil, divided
2 chicken breasts (4 pieces), skinned, boned, cut into 1 inch
    strips
4 to 5 cups assorted greens, washed, drained
1 medium red onion, sliced thin
2 tomatoes, sliced
1/2 cup sliced black olives
Freshly squeezed juice of 2 lemons
2 teaspoons dried oregano
1 1/2 teaspoons dried basil
2 cloves garlic, minced
2 tablespoons capers, drained
1/4 teaspoon each ingredient: salt, freshly ground black
    pepper
1/4 cup freshly grated Parmesan cheese

Italian Chicken Salad

Preheat Burton Stove Top Grill. Brush grill lightly with oil and cook chicken strips over medium-high heat until cooked, about 5 minutes, turning as needed. Chicken will be slightly firm to touch; do not overcook. Remove from grill and reserve.

Divide and arrange greens on individual salad plates. Put onions, tomatoes, olives and chicken strips over greens.

Mix remaining oil, lemon juice, oregano, basil, garlic, salt and pepper. Drizzle over salads. Sprinkle with capers and freshly grated Parmesan cheese. Serve quickly so that the chicken is hot and the salad is cold. Great with bread sticks.

Southwest cooking has become very popular. It is not only very colorful, but also very zestful and tasty. Children and teenagers have become avid consumers of Southwest foods.

SOUTHWEST CHICKEN SALAD

Makes 6 to 8 servings

Dressing

2 cups low-fat, plain yogurt
2 tablespoons chili powder
1 teaspoon each ingredient: ground cumin, garlic powder
1/2 cup chopped cilantro

1 small head lettuce, washed, torn into small pieces
1 red onion, sliced thinly
2 tomatoes, chopped
1 cup sharp longhorn cheddar, shredded
1/4 cup fresh jalapeno peppers, seeded, drained and chopped
     using rubber gloves
1 cup tortilla chips
2 red bell peppers, seeded, cut in 1/2 inch strips
Peanut oil for brushing grill
2 chicken breasts (4 pieces) skinned, boned, cut into 3/4 inch
     pieces

Southwest Chicken Salad

Combine yogurt, chili powder, cumin and cilantro in bowl. Cover and refrigerate until needed.

Place lettuce in large salad bowl. Toss with onions, tomatoes, cheese, jalapeno peppers and chips. Toss with dressing.

Preheat Burton Stove Top Grill. Brush grill surface lightly with oil. Grill peppers over medium-high heat turning frequently until softened. Remove from grill, cut peppers into strips and arrange on top of salad.

Brush chicken with oil, sprinkle with garlic powder and chili powder. Grill over medium-high heat about 5 minutes or until cooked, turning chicken as needed. Chicken will be firm to touch, and juices will run clear when cut with a knife. Remove from grill; place chicken on salads and serve.

CAJUN TURKEY SALAD

Makes 4 to 6 servings

Cajun Spice Mix

1 tablespoon dried minced onions
1 teaspoon cayenne
1/2 teaspoon each ingredient: garlic powder, dried thyme,
   celery salt, salt

3 large slices white turkey meat

1/2 cup chopped walnuts
1 onion, sliced
1/4 cup low-fat, plain yogurt
1/4 cup mayonnaise
3 cups lettuce, shredded in small pieces
1 large tomato, chopped

Combine cajun spices.

Preheat Burton Stove Top Grill. Cook turkey over medium-high heat brushing with cajun spice mix as you grill and turn. Grill about 1 minute on each side. Remove turkey from grill; dice. Place in bowl. Combine walnuts, onion, yogurt and mayonnaise and toss with turkey, lettuce and tomato.

Serve at room temperature or cold.

Combining scallops, shrimp and mushrooms, sprinkled with freshly grated Romano cheese, this dish may serve as a salad, a side dish, or an extremely satisfying meal in itself.

Romano cheese is a sharp and tangy hard cheese which gives a punch to the mildly sweet taste of the shrimp and scallops used in this seafood pasta salad.

LINGUINE WITH GRILLED SEAFOOD

Makes 4 servings

Spinach and Sherry Dressing

2 tablespoons butter or margarine
3 green onions, minced
12 ounces fresh spinach, trimmed, washed, dried
1/2 teaspoon each ingredient: salt, dried tarragon,
        garlic powder
3 tablespoons dry sherry

Peanut oil for brushing grill surface
3/4 pound bay scallops
12 extra large shrimp, peeled, deveined
1/2 pound mushrooms, sliced in half
1 package, 1 pound, linguine, cooked according to
        package directions, drained; arrange
        linguine in bowl

Linguine With Seafood Spinach And Sherry Dressing

2 to 3 tablespoons freshly grated Romano cheese

Heat butter in medium saucepan. Sauté onions until tender, about 5 minutes, stirring often. Stir in spinach, salt and tarragon. Continue cooking 4 to 5 minutes, then mix in sherry. Remove from heat, set aside.

Preheat Burton Stove Top Grill. Brush grill surface lightly with oil. Cook scallops and shrimp over high heat, turning occasionally. Do not overcook; scallops and shrimp will turn opaque and will be slightly firm to touch. Grill mushrooms one minute on each side.

Toss scallops, shrimp, and mushrooms with pasta. Mix with dressing. Sprinkle cheese on top and serve hot.

Monkfish has a sweet, lobster-like taste. I have adapted this recipe from one I enjoyed in New England--lobster chunks on hot dog rolls. This dish can make an excellent luncheon meal.

GRILLED MONKFISH SALAD ON HOT DOG ROLLS

Makes 6 servings

2 tablespoons butter or margarine, melted
1/4 teaspoon garlic powder
1 pound monkfish
1/2 cup mayonnaise
4 ribs celery, minced
4 green onions, minced
1/4 teaspoon each ingredient: garlic powder, salt,
    cayenne
4 hot dog rolls split

Mix melted butter and garlic powder together in a small bowl.

Preheat Burton Stove Top Grill. Grill monkfish over medium-high heat until done, about 4 to 5 minutes. Brush fish with melted butter as you turn it. Monkfish will be opaque and slightly firm to the touch.

Flake grilled fish and place in a bowl. Mix in mayonnaise, celery, onions, garlic powder, salt and cayenne.

Grilled Monkfish Salad On Hot Dog Rolls

Brush rolls with remaining butter and heat on Burton Stove Top Grill, about 30 seconds per side.

Open rolls and mound with monkfish salad. Serve with chips and butter pickles.

Imagine the delicious taste of fresh tuna, grilled to perfection on the Burton grill.

GRILLED TUNA SALAD MEDITERRANEAN STYLE

Makes 4 servings

1 1/4 pound tuna, cut into 3/4 inch strips
1 tablespoon extra virgin olive oil
1/2 teaspoon garlic powder
1 cup boiled potatoes, diced
1 onion, chopped
1 green bell pepper
1 cup green beans, chopped, drained
1/2 cup mayonnaise
1/2 teaspoon each ingredient: dried basil, salt, pepper
4 lettuce leaves
1 tomato, sliced

Preheat Burton Stove Top Grill. Brush tuna with oil. Sprinkle tuna with garlic and cook tuna strips over medium-high heat 2 minutes on each side. Tuna will be firm to the touch and opaque. Do not overcook. Remove tuna to mixing bowl. Flake into small chunks. Mix in potato, onions, pepper, beans, mayonnaise, salt, pepper and basil. Toss lightly.

Arrange lettuce leaf on each plate. Spoon tuna salad onto lettuce leaf; garnish with tomato.

Serve warm or cold with French bread.

For this wonderful fish, vegetable and pasta combination, you may use either left-over seafood, or for a fresher, more elegant taste and appearance, use fresh fish.

In purchasing fresh spinach, always select crisp, dark green leaves. Avoid spinach leaves that are yellow or wilted.

SEAFOOD SPINACH PASTA SALAD

Makes 6 to 8 servings

Dressing

1/2 cup extra virgin olive oil
1/4 cup balsamic vinegar
1/4 teaspoon each ingredient: paprika, dried mustard
1/2 teaspoon each ingredient: garlic powder, salt, pepper
3 tablespoons chopped chives

1 package, 1 pound, spinach pasta, cooked according to
        package directions, drained
1 medium red onion, sliced thinly
1 medium zucchini, cut in half horizontally
3/4 pound haddock fillets
1/2 pound sea scallops
4 tablespoons extra virgin olive oil

Seafood Spinach Pasta Salad

1/2 pound shredded crab meat (you may substitute imitation crab meat)
1 tablespoon sesame seeds, lighted toasted
1 teaspoon dill seed

Blend oil and vinegar in a bowl. Mix in remaining ingredients. Cover and refrigerate until needed. Mix before serving. Set aside.

Place pasta in bowl. Toss with red onions, set aside.

Preheat Burton Stove Top Grill over medium-high heat. Brush cut side of zucchini with oil. Grill 2 minutes per side, cut side of zucchini will brown slightly. Remove from grill, slice and add to salad.

Brush haddock fillets and scallops with oil. Grill haddock fillets 2 minutes per side. Fish will be opaque and flake easily. Remove to plate, flake and add to salad. Grill scallops 2 1/2 minutes per side. Remove to bowl. Toss with shredded crab and add dressing to taste. Serve warm or cold.

Cilantro is the name for coriander, which is a type of Chinese parsley. As a whole seed or ground spice, cilantro is frequently neglected and its inclusion in cooking will add an interesting aromatic dimension to many dishes.

Use thinly sliced flank steak strips for this recipe.

GRILLED FLANK STEAK ON LETTUCE

Makes 4-5 servings

2 tablespoons peanut oil
1 pound flank steak
1/2 tablespoon each ingredient: minced garlic, ground cumin
1 large onion, sliced thinly
2 red bell peppers, seeded, sliced
Juice of 2 limes
1/4 to 1/2 teaspoon red pepper flakes
2 cucumbers, peeled, sliced thinly
1/3 cup minced cilantro

4 large lettuce leaves

Preheat Burton Stove Top Grill over medium-high heat. Brush grill surface lightly with peanut oil.

Cut flank steak into 1 inch strips, against the grain. Sprinkle with garlic powder and cumin. Grill about 6 minutes, turning 2 or 3 times as needed. Meat will be browned on outside and medium well on inside. Toss meat with remaining ingredients.

Grilled Flank Steak On Lettuce

Place 1 lettuce leaf on each plate. Divide salad and spoon onto lettuce leaf. Serve immediately. Good with whole wheat rolls.

The use of cracked mustard seeds produces a spicy, but not overly powerful taste. It is a pleasure to taste this flavored cheese, warm from the grill. This recipe also makes a wonderful appetizer.

WARM CHEESE AND TOMATO SALAD
WITH MUSTARD SEED VINAIGRETTE

Makes 4 servings

Mustard Vinaigrette

3/4 cup extra virgin olive oil
1 clove garlic, minced
6 tablespoons tarragon vinegar
2 tablespoons freshly squeezed lemon juice
1 1/2 tablespoons course mustard
1/2 teaspoon each ingredient: salt, freshly ground black
    pepper

2 large tomatoes, sliced
4 green onions, minced
3 ounces goat cheese, cut into 1/2 inch pieces

Mix oil, garlic and vinegar in bowl. Whisk in juice, mustard, salt and pepper. Cover and refrigerate until ready to serve. Whisk before serving.

Arrange tomatoes on plate, sprinkle with onions.

Warm Cheese And Tomato Salad
With Mustard Seed Vinaigrette

Preheat Burton Stove Top Grill. Over medium heat, place goat cheese on grill and cook until warm but not runny. Turn once. Set cheese on tomatoes. Serve warm.

For this recipe, you may use bell peppers, Melrose peppers or other sweet peppers. You may use a wide variety or combination of spices in the water pan of your Burton grill to add flavor to this salad.

GRILLED PEPPER SALAD

Makes 4 to 6 servings

3 green or yellow bell peppers, seeded
1/4 cup butter or margarine
1 teaspoon dried oregano, divided
1/2 teaspoon each ingredient: garlic powder, thyme
1 onion, sliced thinly

Cut peppers into 1/2-inch strips. Melt butter and mix with oregano, garlic powder and thyme.

Preheat Burton Stove Top Grill. Cook peppers and onions over high heat. Brush with butter mixture. Turn often until vegetables are soft. Remove to serving platter, serve hot.

Garbanzo beans, also known as chickpeas, are widely available either canned or dried

MOROCCAN PASTA SALAD

Makes 4 servings

1 package, 6 or 8 ounces, whole wheat pasta
1 tomato, chopped
1 large onion, chopped
1 can garbanzo beans, drained
1 bunch green onion, trimmed
3 red bell peppers, seeded, cut into thirds
2 tablespoons peanut oil
1 1/2 cups low-fat, plain yogurt
3/4 teaspoon ground cumin
1/2 teaspoon each ingredient: salt, garlic
1/2 cup sliced black olives

Cook pasta according to package directions, drain. Place pasta in deep bowl. Toss with tomatoes, onions and beans.

Preheat Burton Stove Top Grill over medium-high heat. Brush peppers lightly with oil. Grill 1 1/2 minutes per side. Peppers will begin to char. Slice peppers into thin strips.

Place all remaining ingredients into deep serving bowl.

Toss salad with yogurt. Divide salad onto serving dishes. Serve at room temperature or cold with warm pita bread.

Spread sesame seeds on a cookie sheet and toast until light brown, stirring frequently.

Hint: always keep a pair of good quality, sharp scissors solely for use in your kitchen. Scissors are an invaluable kitchen tool.

ORIENTAL SALAD

Makes 4 servings

Sesame Dressing

3 tablespoons soy sauce
2 teaspoons sugar
1/2 cup chicken stock
1/2 teaspoon Oriental sesame oil
2 tablespoons Hoi-sin sauce
1/2 teaspoon each ingredient: garlic, ginger

In small bowl, mix together soy sauce, sugar, chicken stock, sesame oil, Hoi-sin sauce, garlic and ginger; reserve until needed.

1 package, 12 ounces, soft noodles, available at Oriental food
    stores
1 can, 8 ounces, sliced water chestnuts, drained
4 green onions, minced
1 tablespoon peanut oil
1 slice (1/2 pound cooked weight) ham, trimmed of all fat,
    cut into 1/2 inch slices
1/4 teaspoon minced garlic
1 cup snow peas, trimmed

Oriental Salad

Cook noodles in boiling, salted water only until tender, about 2 to 4 minutes. Cut into serving pieces with kitchen scissors. Drain. Place noodles in bowl. Mix in water chestnuts and green onion.

Preheat Burton Stove Top Grill over medium-high heat. Brush grill surface lightly with sesame oil. Sprinkle ham strips with garlic. Grill strips 2 minutes per side or as necessary to heat ham. Remove ham strips and combine with noodles.

Brush grill surface again with sesame oil and heat snow peas, just a few seconds on each side, toss with noodles.

Toss salad with dressing. Arrange salad on plates and serve. Best if served warm.

Cumin is a powerful spice, widely available in both seed and ground form. It is frequently used in spicy dishes, and it can easily dominate a dish in which it is used.

This recipe works equally well as an appetizer or as a side dish.

VEGETARIAN EGGPLANT SALAD
WITH HERBS AND GARLIC

1 large eggplant, cut into 1/4 to 1/2 inch slices
2 tablespoons salt
4 tablespoons extra virgin olive oil, divided
1 onion, sliced
1 large tomato, chopped
1/2 cup green olives
1/2 teaspoon each ingredient: ground cumin, salt, garlic
    powder
1/4 teaspoon pepper

Sprinkle eggplant with salt. Let stand 20 minutes. Wash off salt, pat dry with paper toweling.

Preheat Burton Stove Top Grill over medium heat. Brush eggplant slices with oil. Grill eggplant slices 2 minutes per side. Eggplant slices will be crunchy and golden brown outside and soft on the inside. Remove eggplant from grill and put in food processor fitted with steel blade. Chop.

Vegetarian Eggplant Salad With Herbs And Garlic

Brush onion slices with oil and grill 1 minute per side. Mix eggplant and onion together; chop. Add tomatoes, olives, cumin, salt, garlic powder, pepper and mix.

Spoon onto individual salad dishes and serve warm or cold.

If you refrigerate salad, stir before serving.

GRILLED FRUIT SALAD
WITH GINGER CHUTNEY DRESSING

Makes 4 to 5 servings

Fast Ginger Chutney Dressing
Homemade Ginger Chutney (recipe follows)

1 jar, 7.5 ounces, good quality prepared chutney
1/4 cup chopped candied ginger, available in spice area of most supermarkets
2 cups low-fat, plain yogurt
1/2 cup chopped candied ginger, optional for garnish
2 heads, Bibb lettuce, separated

1 cantaloupe, peeled, seeded, cut into 1 inch wedges
1 pineapple, peeled, cut in 1/2 inch slices
2 bananas, peeled, sliced horizontally
2 apples, peeled, cored, sliced in 1/4 to 1/2 inch pieces
Butter or margarine to brush fruit

Combine chutney, ginger and yogurt. Cover and refrigerate until needed. Stir before serving.

Arrange bib lettuce on plates.

Preheat Burton Stove Top Grill over medium heat. Brush fruit with melted butter. Grill cantaloupe, pineapple and apples about 1 minute on each side. Arrange on salad plate. Grill bananas about 45 seconds on each side. Add to salad plate.

Grilled Fruit Salad With Ginger Chutney Dressing

Spoon dressing over fruit and serve immediately. You may want to serve a scoop of pineapple or orange sherbet in the center of the salad.

GINGER CHUTNEY DRESSING

Makes 3 cups

2 cups dried pears
3 tablespoons candied ginger
1 cup golden raisins
1 small lemon, sliced thinly
1 cup sliced onion
1 1/2 cups firmly packed dark brown sugar
1/2 cup red wine vinegar
3 cloves garlic, minced
1 teaspoon Dijon mustard
1/2 cup tomato sauce
1/2 teaspoon each ingredient: ground cinnamon, ground
      allspice, ground cloves

Wash and chop pears. Combine all chutney ingredients in medium saucepan. Simmer chutney for 20 to 25 minutes. Stir often. Mixture will be thick. Remove from stove and cool. Spoon into covered container.

Dressing

2 cups low-fat, plain yogurt
1 cup chutney

Mix yogurt and chutney together in bowl.

BEEF, PORK, LAMB, VEAL AND HAM

Most of the recipes in this chapter call for the use of a marinade, a sauce, or the use of herbs and spices. These are never intended to disguise or sublimate the taste and nature of the meal itself, but to impart a new, unique, or a flavorful addition to the dish. I intend these flavorings to act as a complement to the meat itself, and the marinades and sauces are light and suggestive rather than overbearing.

In some recipes, I have suggested adding spices to the water pan of the grill. I think you will find that this adds a very satisfying and subtle flavor to the dish. Be imaginative and experimental in flavoring the water when using your Burton Stove Top Grill.

I have also included the recipe and directions for preparing a sukiyaki meal. I strongly recommend cooking this meal at the tableside, using the Burton Stove Top Grill on "Mr. Max" portable burner. This will make the meal more authentic and will provide excitement and color.

This chapter includes recipes from Lemon Veal Cutlets smothered with Shallots and Mushrooms, to Warm Corned Beef on Rye, to Mexican Barbecued Pork and Orange Salad with Jicama.

The term sukiyaki comes from the Japanese "suki" meaning "hoe" and "yaki", meaning "to broil". Japanese peasants are said to have used their hoes, heated over an intense fire, as a grill plate for their meals in the fields.

The ingredients called for in this recipe are available in Oriental food stores. Arrange the sliced ingredients, beautifully and colorfully, on a platter in the kitchen, then cook them at tableside as a dramatic presentation for your family or guests. You'll love it and so will they.

TABLESIDE SUKIYAKI

Makes 4 to 6 servings

Marinade

1/2 cup soy sauce
1/4 cup sugar
1/2 cup sake or dry white wine

1 pound sirloin, chilled
2 packages mung bean threads, 2 ounces each
6 ounces spinach, washed, drained, trimmed, blanched
1 large onion, sliced thinly

1/2 pound medium sized mushrooms, cleaned, cut in half
1 package tofu, 15 1/2 ounces, drained, cut into 3/4 inch
     pieces
2 tablespoons peanut oil

Tableside Sukiyaki

To make the marinade, combine soy sauce, sugar and beef stock in a bowl. Pour marinade into a large seal-sealing plastic bag.

Slice meat, against the grain, into thin strips, about 2 to 3 inches long. Place meat in marinade. Seal the bag securely closed and turn 2 or 3 times to coat the meat. Refrigerate and marinate beef 1 hour. Drain meat, reserve marinade.

Just before serving time, bring a 3/4 full saucepan of water to a boil. Add bean threads, simmer 1 minute. Cut threads into 2 inch long pieces with kitchen scissors. Drain threads.

For tableside grilling, use a tray and arrange the food in decorative rows. Place first the meat, then bean threads, spinach, onion slices, mushrooms and tofu on tray. Bring tray of food to table and have a serving bowl handy. Use a pair of chopsticks to handle the food.

Preheat Burton Stove Top Grill. Cook meat quickly over high heat, turning meat as it cooks with chopsticks. Remove meat to serving bowl. Mix in hot bean threads and spinach. Brush grill surface lightly with peanut oil and grill onion slices and mushrooms. Toss vegetables and stir in remaining meat marinade mixture as they cook. Sprinkle tofu over food.

Serve sukiyaki quickly over hot white rice. Prepare grilled pineapple for dessert (see index for page).

Sake, widely considered to be a Japanese wine, is technically a beer made by the fermentation of rice. Its alcoholic content and its flat taste make it seem comparable to a strong wine.

KOREAN BEEF WITH SAKE MARINADE

Makes 6 servings

Sake Marinade

1/3 cup soy sauce
1/2 cup sake or dry white wine
3/4 cup water
4 green onions, minced
1 teaspoon oriental sesame oil
1 tablespoon sesame seeds
3 tablespoons sugar

1 3/4 to 2 pounds flank steak
2 to 3 tablespoons peanut oil
1/4 teaspoon garlic powder

To make marinade, combine all marinade ingredients in small bowl. Divide the marinade between 2 large self-sealing plastic bags.

Korean Beef Sake Marinade

For best results, partially freeze meat before slicing. Slice the beef into thin 2 inch strips, cutting against the grain. Divide meat between the 2 bags. Seal the bags and turn them a few times to coat the meat. Refrigerate and marinate for 2 to 3 hours, turning bags occasionally. Drain meat.

Preheat Burton Stove Top Grill. Cook meat in a single layer over medium-high heat, turning often. Mix peanut oil with garlic powder. Brush meat with flavored oil as necessary. Beef will brown and will be very tender. Remove meat to serving dish. Serve with rice and Kim Chee (recipe follows).

KIM CHEE

Makes 3 1/2 to 4 cups

1 medium bok choy, sliced thinly into vertical pieces
1 large onion, sliced thinly
2 1/2 tablespoons salt
1 teaspoon crushed red pepper flakes
1/4 teaspoon cayenne
4 cloves garlic, minced
1 tablespoon sugar

Arrange sliced bok choy in a deep ceramic or glass bowl. Sprinkle bok choy with salt. Cover and let stand overnight in refrigerator.

Wash and drain bok choy. Place in a clean bowl. Mix in onion, salt, red pepper flakes, cayenne, garlic and sugar. Cover loosely with wax paper. Weigh down the kim chee using cans of food as the weights. Refrigerate kim chee for 2 to 3 days before serving. Stir once a day. Keep refrigerated. Stir again before serving.

Sesame seeds have a rich, nutty flavor, which is heightened by toasting the seeds for 15 to 20 minutes in a medium oven; stir occasionally until the seeds are golden colored. This marinade is made using toasted sesame seeds and sesame oil.

SKEWERED BEEF WITH SESAME MARINADE

Makes 4 servings

Sesame Marinade

1/3 cup soy sauce
2 teaspoons red vinegar
2 teaspoons Chinese sesame oil
2 cloves garlic, minced
1/8 teaspoon pepper
1 tablespoon lightly toasted sesame seeds
1/2 cup dry white wine or sake

1 1/4 pounds flank steak
12 6-inch bamboo skewers, soaked in water 10 minutes, drained
12 2-inch pieces green onion

To make marinade, combine soy sauce, vinegar, sesame oil, garlic, pepper and sesame seeds in a bowl. Pour marinade into a large self-sealing plastic bag.

Skewered Beef With Sesame Marinade

Cut meat against the grain into thin slices about 2 1/2 x 1/2 inch. Add meat strips to marinade. Seal the bag securely closed and turn 2 or 3 times to coat the meat. Refrigerate and marinate for 2 hours, turn bag occasionally. Drain, discard marinade.

Thread meat onto skewers, using in and out technique. Put a water chestnut on the end of each skewer.

Preheat Burton Stove Top Grill. Grill kabobs over medium-high heat about 3 to 4 minutes, turning occasionally, or until meat is cooked to taste.

Remove kabobs to a serving dish. Serve kabobs hot with Oriental noodles.

SIRLOIN STRIPS WITH RED WINE MARINADE
SERVED ON SOUR DOUGH BREAD

Makes 6 servings

Red Wine Marinade

1 1/2 cups Burgundy wine
3 tablespoons extra virgin olive oil
1/2 teaspoon each ingredient: garlic powder, dried rosemary
2 large shallots, minced
2 tablespoons minced parsley

1 1/4 to 1 1/2 pounds lean sirloin, cut against the grain into
thin 1 to 2 inch strips
Peanut oil to brush grill
1 teaspoon minced parsley
6 slices sour dough bread
Dijon mustard
Dill pickles

To prepare marinade, combine wine, oil, garlic powder, rosemary, shallots and parsley in a bowl. Divide the marinade between 2 large self-sealing plastic bags.

Divide the meat between the 2 bags. Seal the bags securely closed and turn them 2 to 3 times to coat the meat. Refrigerate and marinate for 2 to 3 hours, turning bags occasionally. Drain, discard marinade.

Sirloin Strips with Red Wine Marinade Served On Sour Dough Bread

Preheat Burton Stove Top Grill. Brush meat strips lightly with oil. Grill meat strips over medium-high heat about 3 to 4 minutes, or until done to taste. Meat will brown and be tender. Medium rare works best with this recipe. Remove meat to serving platter. Serve on a slice of sour dough bread with mustard pickles. Allow guests to make their own openface sandwiches.

Carpaccio is an Italian-style dish which employs very thinly sliced strips of high-quality beef, preferably tenderloin, served almost raw. Partially freeze the meat and slice it very thin.

CARPACCHIO STYLE STEAK WITH
MUSTARD MAYONNAISE

Makes 4 to 5 servings

1 cup mayonnaise
1 tablespoon stone ground mustard
1/3 cup freshly grated Parmesan cheese
4 to 5 lettuce leaves
1 large tomato, sliced

1/2 teaspoon freshly ground black pepper
2 tablespoons extra virgin olive oil
1 pound lean beef tenderloin, about 3/4 inch thick, cut into
      3 pieces

1/4 cup minced parsley

Mix mayonnaise with mustard and cheese.

Place 1 lettuce leaf on each plate. Put a dollop of mayonnaise on the side of the plate along with a slice of tomato. Set aside.

Sprinkle meat with pepper.

Carpacchio Style Steak With Mustard Mayonnaise

Preheat Burton Stove Top Grill. Mix pepper with oil. Brush meat. Sear the meat, about 45 seconds on both sides over high heat. Remove meat from the grill. Meat will be charred on the outside and very rare on the inside. Slice meat very thinly. Divide and arrange the meat in a fan design on lettuce. Sprinkle with parsley. Serve carpacchio immediately. Good with dark rye bread and antipasto. This dish can be served as a first course or as a main dish.

Anticuchos is the name for a South American, mainly Peruvian, dish which features strips of lean sirloin marinaded with tart tarragon vinegar, chili flakes and garlic.

ANTICUCHOS WITH TARRAGON MARINADE

Makes 6 servings

Tarragon Marinade

1/4 cup extra virgin olive oil
1 1/2 cups tarragon vinegar
1/2 cup water
1/2 teaspoon chili flakes
2 cloves garlic, minced
1/2 teaspoon salt
1/4 teaspoon freshly grated black pepper

1 1/2 to 1 3/4 pounds lean sirloin steak, cut into 1 inch
    cubes
6 8-inch bamboo skewers, soaked in water 10 minutes,
    drained
Extra virgin olive oil to brush meat
2 tablespoons dried tarragon

To make marinade, combine ingredients in bowl. Pour marinade into self-sealing plastic bag. Add meat, seal the bag securely closed and turn 2 to 3 times to coat the meat. Refrigerate and marinate 3 to 4 hours. Turn bag once or twice while marinating. Drain, discard marinade.

Anticuchos With Tarragon Marinade

Thread meat cubes onto skewers. Brush meat with olive oil. Sprinkle dried tarragon into water in Burton Stove Top Grill. Replace grill surface. Preheat grill. Cook kabobs over medium-high heat until done to taste. Meat will brown on outside and be done to taste on inside after 4 to 5 minutes. Turn meat as needed during grilling to brown all sides. Serve hot with grilled leeks and a bowl of olives.

BEEF STRIPS WITH NUT SAUCE

Makes 6 servings

Nut Sauce

1 1/2 cups chopped walnuts
3/4 cup freshly squeezed lime juice
1/4 cup chicken stock
2 green onions, minced
1/4 teaspoon ground ginger
1 1/2 cups low-fat, plain yogurt

1 1/2 pounds lean sirloin, cut into thin strips, against the
    grain
6 pineapple chunks, drained

6 10-inch bamboo skewers, soaked in water 10 minutes,
    drained

Purée walnuts, juice and stock in food processor fitted with steel
blade. Pour sauce into bowl, reserving 1/2 cup. Mix the
reserved 1/2 cup of nut sauce with yogurt in a second bowl;
cover sauces, set aside.

Thread meat strips using in and out technique. Place a
pineapple chunk at the end of each skewer. Brush with nut
yogurt sauce.

Beef Strips With Nut Sauce

Preheat Burton Stove Top Grill. Cook beef over medium-high heat, 2 to 4 minutes, turning skewer 2 or 3 times as needed. Meat will be browned and cooked to taste. Do not overcook meat. Remove sliced beef to serving dish.

Pass the yogurt nut sauce as a dipping sauce. Good with pilaf or fried rice.

WARM CORNED BEEF ON RYE

Makes 1 sandwich

1/4 cup sauerkraut, drained
1/2 teaspoon caraway seeds
1 4-ounce package sliced corned beef
2 slices rye bread
Stone ground mustard
Whole dill pickles, sliced

Stir sauerkraut with caraway seeds, set aside.

Preheat Burton Stove Top Grill. Heat both sides of corned beef slices, placed on grill surface in a single layer, over medium heat. Heat only until meat is warm. Remove the meat from grill.

Brush one side of a slice of rye bread with stone ground mustard. Place corned beef over mustard. Add sauerkraut and top with remaining slice of bread. Slice sandwich in half and serve with pickles.

Jicama is the root of a Mexican vine and is similar to the potato in consistency. Cut jicama into julienne strips and serve as a vegetable accompaniment with this dish. This vegetable has a delicious chestnut-like taste.

MEXICAN BARBECUE AND ORANGE SALAD
WITH JICAMA

Makes 6 servings

Orange Salad with Jicama

Jicama (recipe follows)

1 3/4 pounds pork tenderloin
6 sweet peppers
1 large red onion, cut into 6 slices

1/2 teaspoon each ingredient: pepper, powdered cumin, garlic powder

3 tablespoons canola oil or peanut oil

Cut pork into 1/2 inch slices. Seed peppers and slice into quarters. Mix pepper, cumin and garlic powder into the oil.

Mexican Barbecue And Orange Salad With Jicama

Preheat Burton Stove Top Grill. Brush pork with flavored oil. Grill pork slices over medium heat, about 1 minute per side. Place pork on serving dish. When you cut into the pork, all pinkness should be gone. Grill peppers and onion slices about 2 minute per side, or until done to taste, brushing as you turn. Remove vegetables and arrange with pork. Serve hot with warm tortillas and tossed salad with jicama.

ORANGE SALAD WITH JICAMA

Makes 6 servings

1 medium head iceberg lettuce
4 medium oranges, peeled, sliced
1/2 cup sliced, pitted black olives
2 tomatoes, chopped

1/4 teaspoon each ingredient: salt, pepper
1/2 teaspoon each ingredient: dried basil, chopped mint
1/4 cup extra virgin olive oil
3 tablespoons red wine vinegar

1/2 pound jicama, peeled
1/2 teaspoon chili powder

Peanut oil for brushing grill

Clean lettuce and tear into bite-sized pieces. Arrange lettuce on 6 salad plates. Arrange orange, olives and tomatoes on lettuce.

Mix salt, pepper, basil and mint together in a bowl with olive oil and vinegar. Drizzle dressing over salad.

Cut jicama julienne and sprinkle with chili powder.

Preheat Burton Stove Top Grill. Brush grill surface lightly with oil. Cook jicama over medium-high heat until warm, turning as necessary so that all sides will be heated.

Divide jicama and sprinkle over salads. Serve warm.

Provençe is a region in southeast France, lying along the Mediterranean Sea. The cooking and tastes of this area have been strongly influenced by both the Mediterranean climate and tradition. Provençal dishes tend to be heavier and heartier than those in other regions of France.

PORK CUTLETS PROVENÇAL

Makes 4 servings

Provençal Sauce

2 tablespoons extra virgin olive oil
1 tablespoon butter or margarine
2 cloves garlic, minced
1 onion, sliced thin
3 large tomatoes, peeled, seeded
1 cup sliced mushrooms
1/4 cup dry white wine
2 tablespoons minced parsley
2 tablespoons capers
2 tablespoons sliced olives, for garnish
1/4 teaspoon each ingredient: salt, dried thyme
1/8 teaspoon fresh ground black pepper
2 bay leaves

1 tablespoon extra virgin olive oil
1/2 teaspoon minced parsley
4 pork cutlets, about 1/2 inch thick

Pork Cutlets Provençal

To make Provençal sauce, heat oil and butter in saucepan over medium heat. Sauté garlic and onion for 4 minutes. Add remaining ingredients and simmer for 3 minutes longer, stirring occasionally. Remove sauce from the heat. Reheat sauce to serve.

Preheat Burton Stove Top Grill. Mix olive oil with parsley. Brush grill surface with flavored oil. Cook cutlets over medium-high heat until all traces of pink have gone and cutlets are browned on the outside. Turn once during grilling. Remove cutlets to individual serving dishes. Drizzle with sauce. Serve with green salad.

This recipe is unique in that no egg is used in the breading. The chops are rolled in corn meal seasoned with spice, which forms a nice crust when grilled.

Serve with mango chutney. Mango chutney provides a wonderful balance of sweet and spicy flavor and is a perfect accompaniment to this and many other meat dishes. You can buy mango chutney or make your own.

PORK CHOPS WITH CORNMEAL BREADING
AND MANGO CHUTNEY

Makes 4 servings

Mango Chutney (recipe follows)

1 1/2 cups cornmeal
2 tablespoons minced parsley
1/2 teaspoon each ingredient: powdered garlic, chili powder
1/4 teaspoon each ingredient: red pepper flakes, dried onion
      flakes

Extra virgin olive oil to brush grill surface

Mix together cornmeal, parsley, garlic, chili powder, red pepper flakes and onion flakes. Arrange cornmeal mixture on a flat plate.

Roll pork chops in cornmeal mixture. Let chops stand for 10 minutes.

Pork Chops With Cornmeal Breading And Mango Chutney

Preheat Burton Stove Top Grill. Brush grill surface lightly with olive oil. Cook pork chops over medium-high heat until all traces of pink are gone on the inside and the meat is crusty on the outside, about 3 to 4 minutes. Turn once during grilling.

Remove chops to individual plates and serve with mango chutney. Good with sliced cucumbers and tomatoes.

NO-COOK MANGO CHUTNEY

Makes about 3 cups

3 large ripe mangoes, peeled, chopped
1 small red onion, minced
2 teaspoons candied, minced ginger
4 1/4 cups freshly squeezed orange juice
1 1/2 tablespoons light brown sugar
1/4 teaspoon each ingredient: ground cloves, ground cinnamon
1/8 teaspoon red pepper flakes

Mix together chopped mangoes, onions, ginger, orange juice, sugar and spices. Let chutney stand 30 minutes. Cover and refrigerate until serving time. Stir and serve.

In this recipe, use crushed garlic cloves in the water pan of the grill. Burton Mesquite Liquid Smoke lends color and a slightly smoky taste to the chops.

Garlic cloves add an aromatic touch to the pork chops.

BARBECUE PORK CHOPS WITH AVOCADO SALAD

Makes 4 servings

Avocado Salad (recipe follows)

Smoky Barbecue Sauce

3 tablespoons peanut oil
1 large onion, minced
3 cloves garlic, minced
4 large tomatoes, chopped
1 can, 8 ounces, tomato sauce
1/2 teaspoon Burton Mesquite Liquid Smoke, optional
3/4 teaspoon ground cumin
1/4 teaspoon each ingredient: salt, fresh ground pepper, red
    pepper flakes
3 tablespoons dark brown sugar
2 tablespoons cider vinegar

4 large cloves garlic, crushed
Peanut oil for brushing grill surface

8 thin pork chops, about 1/2 inch thick, with excess fat
    removed

Barbecue Pork Chops With Avocado Salad

Heat oil in saucepan. Sauté onion and garlic 4 minutes over medium heat, stirring often. Mix in remaining sauce ingredients. Simmer for 10 minutes, stir occasionally. Cool, set aside.

Put crushed garlic cloves in the water pan of the Burton Stove Top Grill. Replace grill surface. Preheat grill over medium-high heat. Brush grill surface lightly with oil. Grill chops about 2 to 3 minutes per side or until pork chops are done to taste and all traces of pink have disappeared. Brush chops lightly with barbecue sauce as you turn them over. Pass extra sauce at the table for guests to enjoy.

Serve with warm tortillas and stewed apples.

AVOCADO SALAD WITH ANCHOVY DRESSING

Anchovy Dressing

1/4 cup extra virgin olive oil
2 tablespoons freshly squeezed lime juice
2 cloves garlic, minced
1/4 teaspoon pepper
1 can, 2 ounces, anchovy fillets, drained, mashed

1 medium head Romaine lettuce, torn into bite-sized pieces
2 tablespoons freshly squeezed lime juice
1 large ripe avocado, peeled, sliced

To make dressing, combine oil, juice, garlic, salt, pepper and mashed anchovies in a small bowl.

Sprinkle lime juice over avocado slices.

To serve, arrange lettuce on 4 chilled salad plates. Set avocado slices decoratively on lettuce. Drizzle dressing over salad. Serve salad chilled.

MIXED GRILL WITH THYME AND MAPLE GLAZED ONIONS

Makes 4 servings

Maple Glazed Onions (recipe follows)

4 shoulder lamb chops, 1/2 inch thick, with excess fat removed
3 3-ounce veal medallions, cut from the loin
Extra virgin olive oil
1 tablespoon chopped fresh thyme leaves
1/4 teaspoon each ingredient: salt, pepper
4 sausage links
1/4 cup red wine (Cabernet)
Fresh thyme for garnish

Brush the lamb and veal with oil, then sprinkle with fresh thyme, salt and pepper.

Preheat Burton Stove Top Grill. Cook lamb, veal and sausage links over medium-high heat. Turn once or twice during cooking. Brown sausage on all sides, until cooked. Test for doneness by cutting into a chop to see if it is the correct stage of doneness for your tastes. Best if slightly pink inside. Grill about 1 1/2 to 2 minutes per side.

To serve, place 1 chop, 1 medallion and 1 link on each plate and garnish with thyme. Serve with maple glazed onions.

MAPLE GLAZED ONIONS

Makes 4 servings

12 small boiling onions, each about 1 inch in diameter
3 tablespoons butter or margarine, cut into 1/2 inch pieces
3 tablespoons maple syrup
1/4 teaspoon salt

Preheat the oven to 400 degrees F.

Cook onions in briskly boiling water, uncovered for 2 minutes. Drain the onions in a sieve or a colander.

With a small, sharp knife, trim the stem ends, slip off the white, parchment-like skins and cut the tops from the onions.

Arrange the onions in a baking dish just large enough to hold them in a single layer. Dot onions with butter. Drizzle onions with syrup. Bake 20 minutes or until onions are tender, stir once or twice to coat onions with syrup. Onions are done when they show no resistance when pierced deeply with the point of a small knife.

Serve hot.

LAMB CHOPS WITH GREEN
TOMATO RELISH

Makes 4 servings

Green Tomato Relish (recipe follows)

1/2 teaspoon each ingredient: powdered garlic, dried thyme, dried rosemary
1/4 teaspoon each ingredient: salt, freshly ground pepper
4 shoulder lamb chops, cut 1/2 inch thick, with excess fat removed

Extra virgin olive oil for brushing grill surface

Combine garlic, thyme, rosemary, salt and pepper. Rub flavoring mixture over lamb chops on both sides.

Preheat Burton Stove Top Grill. Brush grill surface lightly with oil. Cook lamb chops over medium-high heat. Grill, turning once or twice until chops have browned slightly on the outside and are done to taste on the inside. I prefer lamb done with just a hint of pink in the center. You may prefer chops rare or well done. It is up to your individual taste.

Place a chop on each plate and serve with green tomato relish.

GREEN TOMATO RELISH

Makes 3 to 4 cups relish

1 pound green tomatoes, quartered
2 pounds Red Delicious apples, peeled, cored, cut into
    quarters
1 onion, cut into quarters
1/2 cup golden raisins
3/4 cup firmly packed light brown sugar
1/4 cup freshly squeezed orange juice
1 tablespoon red wine
1/4 teaspoon each ingredient: salt, ground nutmeg, ground
    allspice, red pepper flakes, powdered ginger

Chop tomatoes, apples, onion and raisins in food processor fitted
with steel blade. Remove chopped mixture to a saucepan. Mix
in remaining ingredients. Bring mixture to a boil. Reduce heat
to simmer and continue cooking for 30 to 40 minutes, stirring
occasionally. Cool.

Spoon relish into jar and refrigerate until serving time.

Armagnac is an increasingly popular, dark, rich brandy which originates in Gascony in southwest France.

LAMB CHOPS DRIZZLED WITH ARMAGNAC

Makes 4 servings

4 shoulder lamb chops, cut 1/2 inch thick, with excess fat removed
4 tablespoons freshly squeezed orange juice
1 teaspoon dried basil
1/2 teaspoon dried oregano
1/4 teaspoon pepper
1 tablespoon orange zest, for garnish

2 tablespoons Armagnac, or to taste

Set lamb chops in a shallow dish, brush chops with orange juice and sprinkle lamb chops with basil, oregano and pepper. Let chops stand for 1 hour.

Preheat Burton Stove Top Grill. Cook lamb chops over medium-high heat. Grill, turning once or twice until chops have browned slightly on the outside and are done to taste on the inside. Again, I prefer lamb done with just a hint of pink in the center. However, you may prefer chops rare or well done.

Lamb Chops Drizzled With Armagnac

Place a chop on each plate and drizzle the lamb with Armagnac.

Serve hot with stewed prunes and garlic potatoes (see index for page).

Use a sprinkling of rosemary in the water pan of the Burton Stove Top Grill with this recipe. It will serve as an aromatic and give a delicate flavoring to the meat.

CRUMB TOPPED LAMB CHOPS WITH STEWED APPLES AND BLUEBERRIES

Makes 6 servings

Crumb Topping

1/2 teaspoon each ingredient: dried oregano, dried thyme, dried rosemary, salt
1/4 teaspoon fresh ground pepper
3 tablespoons extra virgin olive oil
1 tablespoon dry white wine
2 teaspoons dry mustard
1 1/2 cups fine wholewheat bread crumbs
2 1/2 tablespoons dried rosemary, divided

2 tablespoons extra virgin olive oil
6 loin lamb chops, cut 1/2 inch thick

Prepare topping by mixing together oregano, thyme, rosemary, salt, pepper, olive oil, wine and mustard. Toss herb mixture with crumbs. Spread crumb topping on a flat dish, set aside.

Crumb Topped Lamb Chops With Stewed Apples And Blueberries

Sprinkle 2 tablespoons of remaining rosemary into the water pan of Burton Stove Top Grill. Replace grill surface. Preheat grill. Brush grill surface lightly with oil. Roll chops in crumb topping. Grill chops over medium-high heat. Turn chops over once while grilling. Chops will be crusty on the outside and cooked to taste on the inside. Do not overcook chops. Remove lamb chops and set on individual dishes. Serve hot with stewed apples and blueberries (recipe follows).

STEWED APPLES AND BLUEBERRIES

Makes 6 servings

8 Red Delicious apples, peeled, cored, chopped
2 cups apple cider
2 cups blueberries, washed, picked over
3 tablespoons ground cinnamon
1 1/2 cups sugar
1/2 teaspoon ground nutmeg
2 tablespoons Calvados (apple flavored brandy) optional

Mix apples, apple cider, blueberries, cinnamon, sugar and nutmeg in a saucepan. Bring mixture to a boil over medium heat. Simmer fruit for 15 minutes, stirring occasionally. If mixture becomes too thick, add water by 1/2 cupfuls to desired consistency.

Cool and spoon into bowl. Serve room temperature or cold.

Shish kabob is an Arabic term, "shish", meaning "skewered", and "kabob", meaning "meat".

The marinade for this recipe is made using a balsamic vinegar which is a wine-based, Italian, aged vinegar. This is a truly mellow sweet-and-sour vinegar with an incredible fragrance.

SHISH KABOBS WITH BALSAMIC MARINADE

Makes 4 servings

Balsamic Marinade

1/2 cup extra virgin olive oil
1/4 teaspoon freshly ground black pepper
1/4 cup balsamic vinegar
2 cloves garlic, crushed
1/2 teaspoon dried rosemary
1/4 teaspoon salt

Kabobs

1 1/2 pounds leg of lamb, cut into 3/4 inch cubes
4 medium onions, cut in quarters
16 pieces green pepper, cut into squares
8 cherry tomatoes

4 10-inch bamboo skewers, soaked in water for 10 minutes, drained

Shish Kabobs With Balsamic Marinade

Shallot Sauce

3 shallots, minced
2 cloves garlic, minced
2 tablespoons butter or margarine
2 tablespoons dry white wine
1/2 cup beef stock
1/2 teaspoon dried rosemary

Combine marinade ingredients in bowl.

Divide kabob ingredients and thread onto skewers. Arrange skewers in shallow dish. Pour the marinade over the kabobs and refrigerate for 4 to 6 hours; turn occasionally. When ready to grill, drain marinade.

While kabobs are marinating, prepare sauce. Heat butter in a frying pan. Sauté shallots and garlic for 3 minutes over medium heat. Stir in wine, stock and rosemary. Simmer sauce for 3 minutes. Remove from heat and set aside. Reheat sauce before serving.

Preheat Burton Stove Top Grill. Cook kabobs over medium-high heat turning frequently, about 4 to 6 minutes, until lamb is brown on the outside and done to taste on the inside. Remove skewers to serving dish. Drizzle with hot shallot sauce. Serve hot with rice pilaf.

LEMON VEAL CUTLETS WITH MUSHROOMS AND SHALLOTS

Makes 4 servings

Freshly squeezed juice of 2 lemons
1 1/4 to 1 1/2 pounds veal scallops
1 1/2 cups fine bread crumbs
1 egg or 2 egg whites, slightly beaten
4 tablespoons butter or margarine, melted
1/4 teaspoon each ingredient: salt, white pepper
1/2 pound large mushrooms, cut in half or thirds
3 large shallots, sliced thinly
1/4 cup minced parsley
1 tablespoon lemon zest for garnish
1 lemon, sliced, for garnish

Sprinkle lemon juice over veal scallops, let stand for 1 hour.

Arrange bread crumbs on a flat plate. Roll scallops in crumbs, then dip them in egg and again roll scallops in crumbs.

Preheat Burton Stove Top Grill. Brush grill surface with butter. Cook scallops over medium-high heat about 2 minutes per side or until veal is cooked to taste. Scallops will brown slightly on the outside and be just cooked on the inside. Remove scallops to serving dish. Sprinkle with salt and pepper.

Lemon Veal Cutlets With Mushrooms And Shallots

Brush grill surface with butter. Grill mushrooms and shallots for 1 to 2 minutes. Turn vegetables as needed to warm and lightly brown. Spoon vegetables next to scallops.

Garnish veal with parsley, lemon zest and lemon slices. Serve hot. Good with buckwheat noodles.

Cinnamon used as a flavoring with meats may be new to you, but it adds a pleasant and distinctive taste. Actually, the spice labeled cinnamon is really cassia, which has a more pungent flavor than true cinnamon, making it more suited to meats and curries.

CINNAMON VEAL CHOPS

Makes 4 servings

Cinnamon Marinade

1/2 cup extra virgin olive oil
Freshly squeezed juice of 1 lime
3 tablespoons chopped mint
1/2 teaspoon ground cinnamon

4 veal chops, cut 1/2 inch thick

1 lime, sliced, for garnish

To make marinade, combine olive oil, lime juice, mint and cinnamon in a bowl. Pour marinade into a large self-sealing plastic bag.

Add chops to marinade. Seal the bag securely closed and turn 2 or 3 times to coat the veal. Refrigerate and marinate veal chops 2 to 3 hours. Turn bag occasionally. Drain chops, reserve marinade.

Cinnamon Veal Chops

Preheat grill over medium heat. Grill chops about 2 minutes per side or until veal chops are done to taste and golden brown on the outside. Turn chops once during grilling. Brush chops with reserved marinade as you turn them. Remove veal chops to serving platter. Garnish with lemon slices. Good with spinach and grilled corn.

Veal is often scarce outside of large cities. You may need to order veal ahead from your butcher or meat department if you plan to entertain. When purchasing veal, look for soft, finely-grained, moist flesh that varies in color from off-white to palest pink. The best quality chops are loin chops.

Fresh red currants are available in limited quantities from June through August. Currants are sweet-tart tasting berries which make excellent jams and jellies. My husband raises red currants in his garden, and if he can outsmart the chipmunks, we usually gather enough currants to make this jelly sauce and some jam.

GRILLED VEAL CHOPS WITH RED CURRANTS

Makes 6 servings

6 veal loin chops, cut about 1/2 inch thick

Orange marinade

3/4 cup freshly squeezed orange juice
1/4 cup extra virgin olive oil
1/2 teaspoon ground cinnamon
3 tablespoons minced parsley

Combine juice, oil, cinnamon and parsley. Pour into large self-sealing plastic bag. Add veal chops and turn bag to coat chops. Refrigerate and marinate veal chops 2 to 3 hours. Turn bag occasionaly.

Drain veal chops, reserve marinade.

Grilled Veal Chops With Red Currants

Red Currant Sauce

3 tablespoons butter or margarine
1 small onion, minced
1 1/4 cup chicken stock
3/4 cup red currant jelly
1/4 teaspoon each ingredient: salt, white pepper, cinnamon

1/2 cup fresh currants, (optional) if available, for garnish

Heat butter in saucepan over medium heat. Sauté onion for 4 minutes, stirring often. Add drained marinade and continue cooking until liquid is reduced to about 3 to 4 tablespoons. Mix in chicken stock and jelly. Cook for 4 minutes, stirring often. Season with salt, pepper and cinnamon. Set aside.

Preheat Burton Stove Top Grill. Cook veal chops over medium-high heat, 2 minutes each side. Grill, turning once or twice until chops have browned slightly on the outside and are done to taste on the inside. Do not overcook veal. Cover chops with currant sauce and serve with fresh currants as a garnish.

Curry is customarily thought of as imparting a hot, spicy taste to many varieties of foods. However, there are dozens of quite distinct types of curry available in specialty food shops. Curry powder is made up of a blending of many kinds of spices and herbs, but it is tumeric which gives curry powder a distinctive color and chili powders which control the hotness of curry. For this recipe, use a commercial curry powder. I have used canned fruit combined with curry powder and brown sugar, then baked. This makes a simple, but elegant sauce.

GRILLED HAM WITH CURRIED APRICOTS

Makes 2 servings

Curried Apricots

1 large can, 16 ounces, apricots, drained, discard pits
1/2 cup golden raisins
3 tablespoons butter or margarine, cut in 1/2 inch pieces
1/4 cup firmly packed brown sugar
1 tablespoon curry powder
1/8 teaspoon ground cinnamon
1/2 cup macaroons or other cookie crumbs

1 slice boiled ham, 1/2 inch thick, cut in half
1/4 cup firmly packed dark brown sugar
1 teaspoon Dijon mustard
1 tablespoon red wine vinegar

Grilled Ham With Curried Apricots

Preheat oven to 375 degrees F. To make curried apricots, mix together apricots and raisins in a casserole dish. Sprinkle with butter. Mix sugar, curry powder and cinnamon in a small bowl. Sprinkle apricots with curry mixture and macaroon crumbs.

Bake uncovered for 20 minutes. Stir twice while apricots are baking. Serve warm.

When ready to grill the ham slices, mix together sugar, mustard and vinegar. Sprinkle and press sugar mixture onto ham slices.

Preheat Burton Stove Top Grill. Grill ham slices over medium-high heat about 1 to 2 minutes on each side or until ham is warm and sugar melts. Put a slice of ham on each plate and serve with warm curried apricots.

HAM STEAK WITH RED-EYE GRAVY

Makes 2 to 3 servings

4 tablespoons butter or margarine
Butter or margarine to brush grill

1 slice boiled ham, 1/2 inch thick, cut into 2 inch slices
1/2 cup firmly packed dark brown sugar
1/2 cup strong black coffee

Red-Eye Gravy

Melt margarine in saucepan. Whisk sugar into pan, cook over low heat, stirring constantly until sugar melts. Stir in coffee, simmer 4 minutes. Gravy will be red-brown in color. Set gravy aside.

Preheat Burton Stove Top Grill. Brush grill surface with butter. Grill ham slices over medium-high heat about 1 minute on each side. Ham will brown slightly and be warm. Remove ham to individual plates. Drizzle with hot red-eye gravy. Good with grilled apples and baked beans.

GARLIC STEAK

Makes 2 servings

2 cloves garlic, minced
1/2 teaspoon freshly ground black pepper
Peanut oil for brushing steaks

2 well-trimmed shell steaks or T-bone steaks, cut 1/2 to 3/4
inch thick
1 large clove garlic (use elephant garlic if available), cut
horizontally into slices

Mix garlic and pepper with oil for brushing steaks. Brush steaks with flavored oil.

Cut elephant garlic into thin horizontal slices. Set aside.

Preheat Burton Stove Top Grill. Cook steaks over high heat, 2 minutes per side. Set elephant garlic slices on top of the steaks. Cover grill using the Grill Lid. Reduce heat to medium-high and continue cooking for about 3 to 4 minutes or until steak is done to taste. To test for doneness, remove a steak to a plate. Make a cut into the steak and see if it is done for your individual taste. If not, return steak to grill and continue cooking until done. It may be necessary to turn steak again during grilling. Remove steak to a plate. Serve steaks whole or slice and serve. Serve hot.

PEPPER STEAK

Makes 4 servings

1 flank steak, about 1 to 1 1/2 pounds
2 large red or green bell peppers
1 large onion

1/4 teaspoon each ingredient: garlic powder, dried basil
Peanut oil for brushing meat and vegetables
Salt and pepper to taste

Cut steak into 1/2 to 3/4 inch strips across the grain. Cut the peppers in half, discard the seeds. Slice the peppers into 1/2 inch strips. Slice the onion into 1/2 inch rounds.

Mix the garlic powder and basil into the peanut oil.

Preheat Burton Stove Top Grill. Cook flank steak strips over medium-high heat. Brush meat with flavored oil and turn meat once or twice until cooked to taste, about 2 to 3 minutes per side. Do not overcook. Meat will brown on the outside and be best served rare to medium. Remove steak strips to serving bowl.

Quickly grill pepper strips and onion rings over high heat. Brushing vegetables with flavored oil as you grill. Turn vegetables frequently until they have softened and peppers char slightly.

Toss vegetables with flank steak strips. Season to taste with salt and pepper. Serve hot. Good with brown rice.

SAUSAGES AND BURGERS

I have included this short chapter as a truly fun way to use the Burton Stove Top Grill. These sausage and burger recipes are inexpensive, simple and perfect for children and spontaneous guests. I have also included a recipe for basil potato salad which works as a side dish with all of these sausage and burger meals.

This recipe makes a very easy, but marvelous luncheon dish.

MINIATURE HOT DOGS
WITH MUSTARD AND CURRANT JELLY

Makes 4 servings

1/4 cup Dijon mustard
1 cup currant jelly
1 pound miniature hot dogs
Tooth picks

Combine prepared mustard, currant jelly and 3 tablespoons water in small saucepan. Cook over medium-high heat until mixture is blended, about 3 minutes, stirring often. Cool. Pour sauce in a deep bowl.

Mix in hot dogs, so that all surfaces are coated in mustard sauce.

Preheat Burton Stove Top Grill. Cook hot dogs at medium-high for 3 to 4 minutes, turning once or twice. Hot dogs will be cooked thoroughly and slightly charred on the outside.

Place hot dogs on plate and serve with toothpick. Serve with gherkin pickles and potato salad (recipe follows).

BASIL POTATO SALAD

Makes 6 to 8 servings

6 to 7 large potatoes, about 2 pounds, washed
4 strips lean bacon, cut into thirds
1 medium red onion, minced
1/4 cup cider vinegar
2 tablespoons minced basil
1/4 teaspoon white pepper
3/4 cup mayonnaise

Slide potatoes into boiling salted water and cook over medium heat until potatoes are just fork tender. Run cold water over potatoes, peel and cube. Put potatoes in a deep bowl.

Preheat Burton Stove Top Grill. Cook bacon over medium-high heat, turning as needed. Bacon will be crisp. Remove bacon and crumble. Toss bacon bits and onion with potatoes.

In a separate bowl, mix vinegar, basil, pepper and mayonnaise. Toss potatoes with dressing. Cover, let stand for 1 hour before serving. Toss potato salad again and serve.

This is a recipe from the Alsace province of France. It is another recipe that works wonderfully for football parties.

SMOKED SAUSAGE AND APPLE SLICES ON SAUERKRAUT

Makes 4 to 6 servings

3 cups sauerkraut, drained
1/2 teaspoon caraway seeds
1/4 cup grated carrots
2 large golden or Red Delicious apples, peeled, cored, sliced thinly
1/2 teaspoon each ingredient: salt, dried thyme
1/4 teaspoon pepper
1/2 cup dry white wine
1 pound smoked sausage

Heat sauerkraut in a saucepan over medium heat. Mix in caraway seeds, carrots and apples, stirring often. Add salt, thyme, pepper and white wine; blend all ingredients together. Simmer about 3 minutes. Remove from heat and spread in a casserole dish.

Preheat Burton Stove Top Grill. Cut sausage into approximately 3 inch diagonal pieces, 1/2 inch thick. Cook over medium-high heat about 1 to 1 1/2 minutes on each side. Sausage should be hot and golden brown. Remove sausage, and mix with hot sauerkraut. Serve at once. Good with salad and French bread.

Thyme sprinkled in the water pan adds extra flavor.

GRILLED ITALIAN SAUSAGE

Makes 4 servings

4 mild Italian sausages

Tomato Brushing Sauce

1 can, 8 ounces, tomato sauce
2 tablespoons water
1/2 teaspoon each ingredient: dried marjoram, dried rosemary,
garlic powder, dried oregano
2 tablespoons dried thyme

To make brushing sauce, combine tomato sauce, water, marjoram, rosemary, garlic powder and oregano. Simmer in a saucepan for 4 minutes stirring often. Remove sauce from heat and reserve.

Cut sausages in half horizontally. Preheat Burton Stove Top Grill. Cook sausages over medium-high heat, cut side down, for 2 minutes. Brush liberally with sauce. Turn sausages over, brush with sauce and continue grilling for 2 minutes or until sausages are cooked through. Remove to serving dish. Serve sausages hot with extra sauce and garlic bread. Good also as a first course.

You can easily make this beer mustard, using dry mustard mixed with a small amount of beer. Various types of beers will yield various tastes in the mustard. Experiment to find a beer mustard that you truly enjoy.

BRATWURST WITH BEER MUSTARD

Makes 4 servings

Mustard

6 tablespoons dry mustard
1/3 cup beer
1/4 teaspoon white horseradish, optional

4 bratwurst
1 can beer
4 hot dog rolls
4 pickles, sliced

To make mustard, mix dry mustard, 1/3 cup beer and horseradish together in a small bowl. Let mustard stand for 15 minutes. Stir the mustard before serving. If mustard is too thick, add more beer by the tablespoon until desired consistency.

Cut bratwurst in half horizontally. Pour remaining beer into a bowl. Marinate bratwurst in beef for 1 hour. Drain, discard marinade.

Bratwurst With Beer Mustard

Preheat Burton Stove Top Grill. Cook bratwurst, cut side down, for 2 minutes over medium-high heat. Turn bratwurst over and continue grilling for 2 minutes or until bratwurst are cooked through. Remove from grill.

To serve, place 2 halves of the bratwurst on a warm hot dog roll. Warm rolls, cut side down, on the grill. Serve with pickles, mustard, baked beans and, of course, cold beer.

Pear relish is good to make in the fall and winter when pears are plentiful and cry out for use.

BREAKFAST SAUSAGE WITH PEAR RELISH AND BLUEBERRY BREAKFAST BREAD

Makes 6 servings

Pear Relish

3 firm, ripe pears
3 tablespoons freshly squeezed lime juice
1 cup drained mandarin oranges
1 small red onion, chopped
3 stalks celery, minced
2 teaspoons minced orange zest
1 tablespoon minced mint
1/8 teaspoon red pepper flakes

6 slices prepared breakfast sausages, cut 1/2 inch thick

To make pear relish, core and chop pears. Place in a bowl. Toss pears with lime juice. Add mandarin oranges, red onion, celery, orange zest, mint and red pepper flakes. Toss ingredients lightly. Cover and refrigerate until needed. Pear relish can be made the day before serving.

Breakfast Sausage With Pear Relish And Blueberry Breakfast Bread

Preheat Burton Stove Top Grill. Grill sausage slices 1 1/2 to 2 minutes on each side or until done over medium-high heat. Sausage will be crisp, firm on the outside and cooked through on the inside. Turn sausage once while grilling. Remove sausage to serving plate. Put pear relish on side of plate and serve with sliced blueberry breakfast bread (recipe follows).

BLUEBERRY BREAKFAST BREAD

Makes 8 servings

1/4 cup butter or margarine
3/4 cup sugar
1 egg
2 cups unbleached all-purpose flour, reserve 1/4 cup
1 teaspoon baking powder
1 teaspoon baking soda
1/2 teaspoon each ingredient: salt, ground cinnamon
1/2 cup buttermilk
3/4 cup fresh blueberries, wash, patted dry, or thawed frozen
    berries, drained

Grease a 9 x 9 x 3 inch pan. Preheat oven to 400 degrees F.

Cream butter and sugar together in large bowl of electric mixer.
Beat in egg. Add dry ingredients alternately with buttermilk. Mix
only until batter is smooth.

Toss remaining 1/4 cup flour with blueberries in a bowl. Fold
berries into batter.

Pour batter into prepared pan. Bake for 20 to 25 minutes.

Let bread stand 5 minutes. Remove from pan. Cool blueberry
bread on wire rack. Serve at room temperature.

The use of olives in this recipe gives both the burgers and the salsa quite a new dimension. I think you'll love it.

HAMBURGERS WITH OLIVE SALSA

Makes 4 servings

Olive Salsa

2 medium tomatoes, seeded, chopped
2 cloves garlic, minced
1 small onion, minced
1/4 chopped cilantro
1/8 teaspoon each ingredient: salt, pepper
1/3 cup chopped green olives

1 pound ground beef
1/2 teaspoon powdered garlic
1/4 cup chopped green olives
Salt and pepper to taste

4 sesame seed hamburger rolls
4 lettuce leaves

To prepare salsa, combine tomatoes, garlic, onion, cilantro, salt, pepper and olives in a bowl. Cover and refrigerate until serving time. Toss before serving.

Mix ground beef, garlic, olives, salt and pepper. Shape into 4 hamburger patties about 1/2 inch thick.

Hamburgers With Olive Salsa

Preheat Burton Stove Top Grill. Cook hamburgers, over medium-high heat, about 2 to 3 minutes per side or until done to taste. Burgers will brown on the outside and should be cooked to taste on the inside. Turn burgers once or twice during grilling.

Warm rolls, cut side down, on the grill. Place each roll on a plate. Set a lettuce leaf on the bottom and the burger on top. Serve hamburgers hot with olive salsa on the side.

For best results, grind your own meat or ask your butcher to grind it for you.

LAMB BURGERS WITH FETA CHEESE

Makes 5 to 6 servings

1 pound lean ground lamb
1/2 pound lean ground beef
1 egg
1/2 pita round, ground into crumbs
1 1/2 tablespoons dried oregano
2 cloves garlic, minced
1 small onion, minced
1/2 teaspoon freshly ground black pepper
1/4 cup chopped parsley

6 ounces Feta cheese, crumbled
1/2 cup sliced black olives

Mix lamb and beef with egg, crumbs, oregano, garlic, onion, pepper and parsley. Shape into 6 burgers. Chill until ready to grill.

Preheat Burton Stove Top Grill. Grill burgers over high heat until golden brown on the outside and medium done on the inside or to taste. Turn burgers as necessary.

Remove lamb burgers to serving dish. Sprinkle with crumbled feta cheese and olives. Serve burgers hot with warm whole wheat pita bread.

GERMAN MEATBALLS

Makes 4 to 6 servings

3/4 pound each, ground pork, ground veal
1 egg, slightly beaten
3/4 cup fine bread crumbs
1 medium onion, minced
1 teaspoon lemon zest
1/2 teaspoon each ingredient: salt, dried tarragon
1/4 teaspoon fresh ground pepper

Sauce

2 cups beef stock
1 tablespoon freshly squeezed lemon juice
2 tablespoons cornstarch
1/4 cup capers, drained

Mix pork and veal together in a deep mixing bowl. Blend in egg, bread crumbs, onion, lemon zest, salt, tarragon and pepper. Shape into 2 inch patties. Place on dish and refrigerate until ready to grill.

Heat stock until just simmering over medium heat. Remove 2 tablespoons stock and combine with lemon juice and cornstarch. Return mixture to stock and continue simmering until sauce thickens. Stir in capers.

German Meatballs

Preheat Burton Stove Top Grill. Cook meatball patties about 4 to 5 minutes over medium-high heat, turning once. Meat will be crusty on the outside and cooked to taste on the inside.

Ladle sauce over patties on serving dish. Good served hot with red cabbage, grilled apples and pumpernickel bread.

CHEESEBURGERS

Makes 4 servings

1 pound ground beef
1 egg
1/2 cup bread crumbs
1 tablespoon mustard
1/4 teaspoon pepper
4 slices American cheese
4 hamburger rolls, warmed on the grill

Combine beef, egg, bread crumbs, mustard and pepper. Shape into 4 patties.

Preheat Burton Stove Top Grill. Cook burgers over medium-high heat. Turn once or twice until rare. Add a slice of cheese on top of each burger. Cook 1 minute longer. Serve hot burgers on rolls.

CHICKEN AND TURKEY

Both the cost and the versatility of chicken make it one of the most popular entrées. Recently, the concern for lowered-fat foods has added another positive aspect to the grilling and enjoyment of both chicken and turkey dishes.

The fast-cooking nature of the Burton Stove Top Grill lends itself to the use of chicken breasts, kabobs, strips and wing recipes. They are tender and delicious, and they cook evenly and thoroughly.

One new concept I have employed in this chapter with several recipes is the use of citrus or herbs cooked under the skin of chicken breasts. Select chicken breasts with the skin still on the breast. Separate the skin from the breast with your fingers. Slide fruit slices or herbs under the skin and grill with the skin on. This gives a terrific flavor to the chicken breast.

In this chapter, enjoy recipes from Chicken Kabobs with Peach Glaze, to Chicken Fajitas, to Chicken Breasts with Lime Slices Under the Skin.

This sandwich has gained immense popularity recently. It has been added to many menus from fast food restaurants to gourmet sandwich shops. It can be made simply, quickly and deliciously at home using the Burton grill.

GRILLED CHICKEN BREAST SANDWICH

Makes 4 servings

Brushing Sauce

1/2 cup chili sauce
2 tablespoons molasses
1/2 teaspoon dry mustard
2 tablespoons freshly squeezed orange juice

2 whole chicken breasts, skinned, boned

4 burger buns or rolls, sliced
4 leaves of lettuce
4 slices tomato
1 onion, sliced thinly
Sliced pickles

Grilled Chicken Breast Sandwich

Brushing Sauce

Combine chili sauce, molasses, mustard and orange juice in a bowl.

Flatten chicken pieces between 2 sheets of waxed paper, using a spatula or mallet. Arrange chicken in a flat glass bowl, brush with sauce.

Preheat Burton Stove Top Grill. Cook chicken over medium-high grill until done, turning once. Cook chicken 3 to 5 minutes. Chicken will be slightly firm to the touch. Remove chicken from grill.

Arrange lettuce leaf on bottom side of bun. Put chicken breast on lettuce. Top chicken with tomato slice and onion rings. Serve hot with pickles.

Wing tips can be saved, frozen, and used in future chicken stock preparation.

NEW YORK STATE CHICKEN WINGS WITH BLUE CHEESE DIPPING SAUCE

Makes 4 servings

Blue Cheese Dipping Sauce

1 cup mayonnaise
3 cloves garlic, minced
1 small onion, minced
1/4 cup minced fresh parsley
1/2 cup sour cream or low-fat, plain yogurt
1 tablespoon freshly squeezed lemon juice
1 tablespoon white sugar
1/3 cup crumbled blue cheese, or to taste
Salt and freshly ground black pepper to taste
1 bunch of celery, trimmed, cut into celery sticks

Chicken Wings

2 dozen chicken wings
Salt and pepper

Hot Sauce

2 tablespoons peanut oil
2 tablespoons hot sauce
1 tablespoon white vinegar

New York State Chicken Wings
With Blue Cheese Dipping Sauce

Mix together mayonnaise, garlic, onion, parsley, sour cream, lemon juice, vinegar, cheese, salt and pepper in a bowl. Cover and refrigerate until serving time. Stir before serving.

Remove and discard the tip of each chicken wing. Cut the main wing at the joint, yielding 2 pieces each wing. Sprinkle wing pieces with salt and pepper.

Preheat Burton Stove Top Grill to medium-high heat. Brush grill surface lightly with peanut oil. Cook chicken wings, 5 to 6 minutes, turning as necessary. Cover grill with Grill Lid after 2 minutes of grilling. Wings are done when crusty on outside and juices run clear when cut with a knife. Remove wings from grill and arrange on serving dish.

Heat oil in small saucepan. Blend in hot sauce and vinegar. Remove pan from heat. Pour hot sauce over chicken wings. Serve chicken wings hot with celery sticks and blue cheese dipping sauce.

CHICKEN WITH ORANGE SLICE UNDER THE SKIN

Makes 4 servings

Orange Marinade

1/3 cup extra virgin olive oil
1/4 cup freshly squeezed orange juice
1 clove garlic, minced
1/2 teaspoon dried rosemary
1/4 teaspoon cayenne
2 tablespoons minced parsley

**2 whole chicken breasts, leave skin intact, boned, cut into 4
        pieces**
1 orange, cut into 4 very thin slices
1/4 cup minced parsley for garnish

Orange Marinade

Combine olive oil, orange juice, garlic, rosemary, cayenne and parsley. Pour marinade into self-sealing plastic bag. Add chicken breasts, close bag securely and turn several times, so that all areas of chicken are coated by marinade. Refrigerate and marinate chicken for 1 hour. Drain, discard marinade.

Chicken With Orange Slice Under The Skin

Loosen skin on chicken breast. Slide in 1 thin slice of orange between skin and chicken. Pat skin back into position.

Preheat Burton Stove Top Grill. Cook chicken, skin side down, over medium-high grill for 4 to 6 minutes, turning once. Chicken is done when juices run clear when cut with a knife. Remove chicken from grill and place on individual dishes. Sprinkle with parsley. Serve hot with wild rice salad (recipe follows).

Wild rice salad works well here as a side dish. It can be prepared ahead of time, and it works well served warm or cold.

WILD RICE SALAD

Makes 6 to 8 servings

4 cups chicken stock
1 cup wild rice
1 1/2 cups long-grain white rice
2 cups chopped red bell pepper
1/2 cup safflower oil
1/4 cup red wine vinegar
1 tablespoon Worcestershire sauce
1/4 teaspoon freshly ground pepper
3 cups water
1 cup fresh peas
1 large red Spanish onion, sliced, separated into single rings

Place stock in large sauce pan and bring to a boil over high heat. Stir in wild rice and bring once again to a boil. Cover, reduce heat to low and simmer 40 minutes. Stir white rice into mixture and continue to simmer 15 to 20 minutes or until all liquid is absorbed. Remove from heat and let cool.

Place cooled rice mixture in large serving bowl. Mix in red pepper.

In a small bowl, whisk oil, vinegar, Worcestershire sauce and pepper together. When completely blended, pour over rice mixture and toss.

Wild Rice Salad

Bring water to a boil in a small sauce pan. Put peas into water, and cook for 1 minute or until peas turn bright green. Drain peas into a strainer and immediately rinse under cold running water. Arrange peas in a circular wreath atop rice mixture. Place onion rings in center of pea wreath. Serve warm or cold.

CHICKEN WITH BRANDY SAUCE

Makes 4 servings

Processor Brandy Sauce

1/4 cup brandy
1 egg
1 teaspoon orange zest
2 tablespoons freshly squeezed orange juice
1/2 cup butter or margarine, melted
1/4 teaspoon salt
1/8 teaspoon white pepper
1/2 cup whipped cream

2 chicken breasts, leave the skin intact, boned, cut into 4
   pieces
2 tablespoons butter or margarine to brush chicken

To make the sauce, blend all ingredients in a food processor fitted
with a steel blade. Set aside on a warmer or in very low oven.

Chicken With Brandy Sauce

Brush chicken with butter.

Preheat Burton Stove Top Grill. Cook chicken over medium-high heat for 5 to 6 minutes, skin side down. Turn once during grilling. Chicken is cooked when it is firm to the touch and when the juices run clear when cut with a knife.

To serve, place a chicken piece, skin side up, on each plate, and drizzle with sauce. Serve hot. Good with French bread and wild rice salad (see index for page).

It is difficult to determine if the bay leaves, which are commonly sold bottled or boxed in the spice sections of supermarkets, are very old. However, old, dried bay leaves will have lost their flavor, making them ineffective as a flavoring. You may be able to obtain fresh bay, which will be very strongly scented. Bay leaves should always be discarded before serving a dish.

SPANISH STYLE CHICKEN

Makes 4 servings

Raisin Wine Sauce

2 tablespoons extra virgin olive oil
2 tablespoons butter or margarine
1 large onion, chopped
1/2 pound mushrooms, sliced
2 tablespoons unbleached all-purpose flour
3/4 cup dry white wine
3/4 cup chicken stock
1 1/2 tablespoons freshly squeezed lemon juice
2 bay leaves
1/4 teaspoon each ingredient: dried thyme, salt, pepper
1/2 cup raisins

1/2 teaspoon dried thyme
Extra virgin oil to brush chicken
2 whole chicken breasts, skinned, boned, cut in 1/2 inch strips

Spanish Style Chicken

Raisin Wine Sauce

Heat oil and butter in saucepan. Sauté onion and mushrooms for 4 minutes over medium heat, stirring occasionally. Stir in flour and continue cooking 2 minutes. Stir in white wine and chicken stock; bring mixture to a boil. Simmer sauce, stirring constantly until sauce thickens. Mix in juice, bay leaves, thyme, salt, pepper and raisins. Simmer 5 minutes. Taste to adjust seasonings. Remove from heat; discard bay leaves.

Preheat Burton Stove Top Grill. Stir thyme into oil. Brush chicken strips with flavored oil. Grill chicken over medium-high heat about 3 minutes on each side, or until done to taste. Chicken is done when it is slightly firm to the touch and juices run clear when cut with a knife.

Remove chicken to individual plates. Drizzle hot sauce over chicken. Serve hot. Serve with gazpacho and flan for dessert.

Sage marinade will have a powerful and aromatic quality.

CHICKEN BREASTS WITH MUSHROOMS

Makes 4 servings

Mushroom Cornbread (recipe follows)

Sage Marinade

1/2 cup extra virgin olive oil
1/4 cup freshly squeezed lemon juice
1/2 teaspoon dried sage
2 bay leaves
1/2 cup yellow cornmeal

2 whole chicken breasts, leave skin intact, boned, cut into 4
    pieces
3/4 cup sliced mushrooms
1/2 teaspoon dried sage

To make marinade, combine olive oil, lemon juice, sage and bay leaves. Pour marinade into self-sealing plastic bag. Add chicken breasts and seal the bag securely closed. Turn bag a few times so that all portions of chicken are coated by the marinade. Refrigerate and marinate for 1 hour. Drain, discard marinade.

Chicken Breasts With Mushrooms

Separate skin from chicken. Toss mushrooms with sage. Slide mushrooms under the skin. Replace skin.

Preheat Burton Stove Top Grill. Cook chicken over medium-high heat, skin side down, for about 5 minutes, turning once. Chicken will be slightly firm to the touch and juices will run clear when chicken is cut with a knife.

Remove chicken to serving dish. Serve chicken hot with mushroom cornbread.

This side dish of cornbread is very easy to make and is an all-time favorite.

MUSHROOM CORNBREAD

Makes 6 servings

3 lean bacon slices, cut in half
6 tablespoons butter or margarine, melted, divided
3/4 cup yellow cornmeal
1/4 cup unbleached all-purpose flour
2 tablespoons baking powder
1/2 teaspoon each ingredient: baking soda, salt
1 egg
1/2 cup buttermilk
1 cup sliced mushrooms

Grease an 8 x 8 inch baking pan. Set aside. Preheat oven to 400 degrees F.

Preheat Burton Stove Top Grill. Cook bacon strips over medium-high grill until crisp, turning bacon as needed.

Crumble bacon and place in a non-stick frying pan. Heat 2 tablespoons of butter. Add mushrooms and sauté over medium heat until tender, stirring often, about 5 minutes.

Mushroom Cornbread

Mix the cornmeal, flour, baking powder, baking soda and salt in a bowl. Blend in egg, buttermilk and rest of butter. Do not overheat. Mixture should be just combined. Mix in mushrooms.

Spoon batter into prepared pan. Bake 18 to 20 minutes. Inserted bread tester will come out dry. Cool cornbread on wire rack. Cut cornbread into 6 pieces.

Make this salsa to your own taste; you can make it spicier or hotter to suit your own family or company. Salsa makes a marvelous sauce for a wide variety of chicken dishes.

For the side dish of refried beans, fry the bacon on your Burton grill. It cooks the bacon perfectly, while removing much of the excess bacon grease.

CHICKEN SPEARS WITH AVOCADO SALSA

Makes 4 servings

Avocado Salsa

1 large ripe avocado, peeled, discard pit
Freshly squeezed juice of 2 limes
2 medium tomatoes, cut in half, seeded, chopped
4 green onions, minced
1 green bell pepper or 2 mild Melrose peppers, seeded, chopped
1/4 cup minced cilantro
2 tablespoons extra virgin olive oil
1/2 teaspoon ground cumin
1/4 teaspoon each ingredient: salt, red pepper flakes

2 whole chicken breasts, skinned, boned, cut into 4 pieces
16 bamboo skewers, soaked in water 10 minutes, drained
1/2 cup freshly squeezed lime juice
1/4 cup extra virgin olive oil
1/2 teaspoon ground cumin
1/4 teaspoon red pepper flakes

Chicken Spears With Avocado Salsa

To prepare avocado salsa, dice avocado and toss with lime juice in a bowl. Mix in tomatoes, green onions, pepper and cilantro. Toss salsa ingredients with olive oil, cumin, salt and red pepper flakes. Cover lightly and refrigerate until serving time. Toss salsa again before serving. Taste to check seasonings.

Cut each chicken piece into 4 strips. Thread chicken onto skewers. Place in a flat dish. Mix juice, olive oil, cumin and red pepper flakes. Brush chicken with marinade. Let chicken marinate for 1 hour. Drain, discard marinade.

Preheat Burton Stove Top Grill. Cook chicken skewers over medium-high grill for about 6 minutes or until chicken is cooked, turning as needed.

Chicken is done when it is slightly firm to the touch and juices run clear if the chicken is cut with a knife. Serve with tortillas and refried beans (recipe follows).

REFRIED BEANS

Makes 4 to 6 servings

1 pound dried red kidney beans
5 strips lean bacon, cut in half
1 pound dried red kidney beans
1/2 teaspoon each ingredient: ground cumin, salt, garlic
      powder
1/4 teaspoon each ingredient: pepper, red pepper flakes

Wash beans and place in a large pot. Cover beans with water and bring to a boil. Reduce heat to a simmer and continue cooking for 2 1/2 to 3 hours, uncovered. Add more water, if necessary, and stir the beans occasionally. Beans can be prepared the day before serving. Set aside 1 1/2 cups of the cooking liquid separately from the beans.

Preheat Burton Stove Top Grill. Cook bacon over medium-high heat, turning until done to taste. Drain bacon on paper towels. Crumble bacon. Purée beans using a food processor fitted with a steel blade or use a potato masher.

Heat the reserved cooking liquid and bacon in a large pan. Mix in the beans and seasonings. Cook over medium heat until beans are hot. Remove beans from heat.

When ready to serve, heat refried beans in a frying pan, stirring often.

Green olives are picked unripe and pickled in brine. They impart a tart taste to the chicken and add color and character to the dish.

CHICKEN WITH GREEN OLIVES

Makes 4 servings

Green Olive Sauce

1 tablespoon extra virgin olive oil
1 tablespoon butter or margarine
2 cloves garlic, minced
1 small onion, minced
1 green bell pepper, seeded, chopped
1 can, 8 ounces, tomato sauce
1/2 teaspoon Worcestershire sauce
1/4 teaspoon each ingredient: red pepper flakes, salt,
    sugar
1/2 cup sliced green olives

2 whole chicken breasts, skinned, boned, cut into 4 pieces

Green Olive Sauce

Heat oil and butter in saucepan. Sauté garlic, onion and pepper for 5 minutes, stirring often. Stir in tomato sauce, Worcestershire sauce, red pepper flakes, salt, sugar and green olives. Simmer 5 minutes. Remove from heat.

Chicken With Green Olives

Flatten each piece of chicken between 2 sheets of waxed paper with a mallet or spatula. Brush chicken liberally with green olive sauce.

Preheat Burton Stove Top Grill. Cook chicken over medium-high heat for 4 to 5 minutes, turning once or until chicken is cooked. Brush chicken with sauce as you turn it. Chicken is cooked when chicken meat is firm to touch and cooked through, and all traces of pinkness are gone. Remove to individual dishes.. Serve with hot sauce. Good with saffron rice and cornbread.

The use of the herb stuffing gives a wonderful flavor to the chicken breasts and keeps them particularly moist and juicy.

CHICKEN WITH HERBS

Makes 4 servings

Herb Stuffing

2 cups fine bread crumbs
2 tablespoons minced parsley
**1/2 teaspoon each ingredient: dried basil, dried tarragon,
     dried thyme**
1/4 teaspoon each ingredient: salt, pepper

2 whole chicken breasts, leave skin intact, boned,
Extra virgin olive oil for brushing chicken

Herb Stuffing

Toss bread crumbs with parsley, basil, tarragon and dried thyme.

Loosen skin over chicken. Lightly spoon about 1/4 cup of the stuffing under the skin. Replace skin over chicken. Brush each chicken breast with oil.

Preheat Burton Stove Top Grill. Grill chicken breasts, over medium-high heat, skin side down for 4 minutes. Turn chicken breasts over and continue grilling for 3 minutes or until chicken is done. Chicken is done when it is slightly firm to the touch and juices run clear if the chicken meat is cut with a knife. Serve hot with ratatouille or grilled zucchini as a side dish.

The limes should be sliced thinly. After grilling, discard the chicken skins and use fresh slices of lime as a garnish.

CHICKEN BREAST WITH LIME SLICES UNDER THE SKIN

Lime, Coriander, Yogurt Sauce

1 teaspoon lime zest
2 tablespoons freshly squeezed lime juice
1/2 cup minced coriander
2 cups low-fat, plain yogurt

1 small lime, cut into 4 paper thin slices
Butter or margarine to brush chicken
2 whole chicken breasts, leave skin intact, boned, cut into 4
pieces

Yogurt Sauce

Blend the zest, juice and coriander into the yogurt. Spoon sauce into a serving bowl. Cover and refrigerate until serving time. Stir sauce before serving.

Chicken Breast With Lime Slices Under The Skin

Preheat Burton Stove Top Grill. Loosen the skin over chicken. Slide 1 thin slice of lime under the skin. Replace skin over chicken. Brush butter over chicken. Grill chicken over medium-high heat, skin side down for 3 to 4 minutes. Turn chicken over and continue grilling for 2 to 3 minutes or until chicken is done. Chicken is done when it is slightly firm to the touch and juices run clear if cut with a knife.

Serve chicken hot, drizzled with yogurt sauce.

These fajitas are made using spiced, grilled chicken strips, which are wrapped in warm tortillas. They will be especially popular with children and guests of all ages.

CHICKEN FAJITAS

Makes 4 servings

Brushing Sauce

4 green onions, minced
1 teaspoon garlic powder
6 tablespoons dark brown sugar
5 tablespoons red wine vinegar
1 1/2 cups light beer
3 teaspoons prepared mustard

2 whole chicken breasts, skinned, boned, cut into 1 inch strips
4 flour tortillas
1/2 cup chopped cilantro

Brushing Sauce

Combine onions, garlic, sugar, vinegar and beer in a saucepan. Simmer 4 to 5 minutes, stirring occasionally. Remove from heat.

Place chicken strips in a shallow glass dish. Brush chicken liberally with sauce. Let stand for 1 hour.

Chicken Fajitas

Preheat Burton Stove Top Grill. Cook chicken strips over medium-high heat for 5 to 6 minutes, turning as needed, or until chicken is slightly firm to the touch and juices run clear when cut with a knife. Remove strips to a bowl.

Brush onion slices with oil and grill for about 45 seconds to 1 minute on each side.

To serve, warm tortillas, on each side over hot grill. Lay tortilla flat, place chicken strips in center, sprinkle with onions and cilantro. Roll tortillas and serve hot. Good with refried beans.

The use of yogurt has gained tremendous popularity in recent years. This yogurt marinade serves to moisturize the chicken and adds a subtle, but distinctive flavor.

Cardamon is member of the ginger family and is native to southern Asia. It is the dried seed pods of the cardamon plant which are sold in stores as cardamon.

CASHEW CHICKEN WITH YOGURT MARINADE

Makes 4 servings

Yogurt Marinade

1 cup low-fat, plain yogurt
2 teaspoons minced fresh ginger
1/4 teaspoon each ingredient: white pepper, ground cardamon, ground allspice

Cashew Sauce

2 tablespoons butter and margarine
1 small onion, minced
2 cloves garlic, minced
1/2 cup roasted cashews
1/4 teaspoon each ingredient: ground cardamon, chili powder, turmeric
1 1/2 cups low-fat, plain yogurt

Cashew Chicken With Yogurt Marinade

2 chicken breasts, leave skin intact, boned, cut into 4 pieces
1/2 cup chopped cashews for garnish

To prepare yogurt marinade, combine yogurt, ginger, pepper, cardamon and allspice in a bowl. Spoon into a self-sealing plastic bag. Add chicken pieces and seal the bag securely closed. Turn the bag several times so that all areas of the chicken are coated by the marinade. Refrigerate and marinate for 1 1/2 hours. Drain, discard marinade.

Meanwhile, to prepare the cashew sauce, heat the butter in a saucepan. Sauté onion, garlic, nuts and spices for 5 minutes, stirring occasionally. Cool. Purée mixture in a small or regular food processor fitted with steel blade. Blend mixture into yogurt. Stir to combine ingredients. Set aside until needed.

Preheat Burton Stove Top Grill. Cook each chicken piece over medium-high heat, skin side down first, for about 5 minutes, turning chicken pieces once during grilling. Chicken is done when it is slightly firm to the touch and juices run clear when chicken is cut with a knife. Remove chicken pieces to individual plates. Drizzle chicken with warm cashew sauce.

Sprinkle with chopped cashews. Serve chicken hot with rice.

I have used fresh peaches to make this glaze. Always choose firm, bright-colored peaches; avoid green or very firm, hard peaches. They are immature and will not ripen well.

For chicken kabobs, cut chicken into small pieces.

CHICKEN KABOBS WITH PEACH GLAZE

Makes 4 servings

Peach Glaze

2 cups peach juice
1/2 teaspoon curry powder
**1/4 teaspoon each ingredient: ground cinnamon, chili powder,
     ground allspice**
2 tablespoons cornstarch

4 bamboo skewers, soaked in water 10 minutes, drained
4 peaches, cut into quarters
4 green onions, cut into 2 inch lengths
2 green bell peppers seeded, cut into 2 inch pieces
**1 pound boneless, skinless chicken breast, cut into 1 inch
     pieces**

Peanut oil to brush grill surface

Chicken Kabobs With Peach Glaze

To make peach glaze, heat peach juice to a boil in saucepan. Mix in curry powder, ground cinnamon, chili powder and ground allspice. Remove 3 tablespoons of the juice, mix with cornstarch. Return cornstarch mixture to saucepan. Reduce heat and simmer about 4 to 5 minutes or until sauce thickens. Remove from heat. Set aside.

Thread skewers alternately with pieces of peach, green onions, pepper and chicken cubes. Brush each kabob generously with peach glaze.

Preheat Burton Stove Top Grill. Brush grill surface lightly with peanut oil. Grill kabobs over medium-high heat, rotating every 2 minutes until done to taste. Chicken should be slightly firm to the touch and cooked through. Remove kabobs to serving dish. Serve hot with noodles.

I have included six Oriental chicken recipes which I have grouped together here for use with the Burton grill. These are Oriental in style, taste and character.

You may use either of the two major types of peanuts, Spanish or Virginia, for this recipe. The red pepper flakes called for here may be used liberally or conservatively, according to your own desire for fiery flavoring.

SPICY CHICKEN WITH GREEN PEPPER AND PEANUTS

Makes 4 servings

Marinade

2 egg whites, slightly beaten
1 tablespoon cornstarch
1/4 teaspoon each ingredient: salt, garlic powder
1/8 teaspoon white pepper

2 chicken breasts, discard skin, boned, cut into 4 pieces
Peanut oil for brushing grill surface

Spicy Chicken With Green Pepper And Peanuts

Sauce

3 tablespoons peanut oil
2 cloves garlic, minced
1/2 teaspoon freshly grated ginger root
1/4 teaspoon red pepper flakes
4 green onions, cut in half horizontally and then into 1 inch
    pieces
1 can sliced bamboo shoots, drained
1 cup sliced green bell pepper strips
1/2 cup unsalted roasted peanuts
3 tablespoons soy sauce
2 tablespoons dry white wine
1/2 teaspoon sugar

To make marinade, combine egg whites, cornstarch, salt, garlic and pepper. Place in shallow bowl. Add chicken pieces. Refrigerate for 1 hour.

While chicken is marinating, prepare sauce. Heat oil. Sauté garlic, ginger and red pepper flakes in saucepan for one minute. Add green onions and continue cooking over medium-high heat for 2 minutes, stirring often. Mix in bamboo shoots, pepper strips and peanuts; cook for 1 minute. Stir in soy sauce, wine and sugar. Cook until sauce is hot and ingredients are combined. Remove from heat and reserve.

Spicy Chicken With Green Pepper And Peanuts

Preheat Burton Stove Top Grill. Slice each chicken piece into 4 or 5 strips. Brush grill surface lightly with oil. Cook chicken strips for about 4 or 5 minutes over medium-high heat. Turn chicken strips once or twice during grilling. Chicken is done when it is slightly firm to the touch and juices run clear when chicken strips are cut with a knife. Remove chicken strips and mound in the center of serving dish. Top with hot sauce. Serve at once. Good with rice or noodles.

Coconut is a very important ingredient in Southeast Asian cooking. Coconut meat is available fresh, in jars and cans in Oriental specialty shops.

THAI CHICKEN KABOBS WITH COCONUT SAUCE

Makes 4 servings

Coconut Sauce

1 cup canned, unsweetened coconut milk
1 teaspoon ground curry
1/2 cup smooth peanut butter
1/4 cup sugar
3 tablespoons white vinegar
2 tablespoons cornstarch

2 whole chicken breasts, skinned, boned, cut into 1 inch
    pieces
1 cup freshly squeezed lime juice
1 teaspoon lime zest
4 8-inch bamboo skewers, soaked in water for 10 minutes,
    drained
1/4 cup freshly grated coconut, for garnish

Peanut oil to brush chicken and grill surface

Thai Chicken Kabobs With Coconut Sauce

To prepare coconut sauce, blend coconut milk and powdered curry together in a saucepan. Bring to a boil. Reduce heat to a simmer and blend in peanut butter, sugar and vinegar mixed with cornstarch. Simmer until smooth, about 2 minutes, stirring often. Sauce will thicken slightly. Remove from heat. Serve sauce hot.

Marinate chicken pieces in freshly squeezed lime juice and lime zest for 1 hour. Drain chicken and thread onto skewers. Brush chicken kabobs with peanut oil.

Preheat Burton Stove Top Grill. Brush grill surface lightly with oil. Grill chicken kabobs over medium-high heat for about 3 to 4 minutes, turning as necessary to cook all sides of kabobs. Chicken is done when slightly firm to touch and juices run clear when cut with a knife.

Place a chicken kabob on each plate, drizzle with coconut sauce and serve with white rice or fried rice. Garnish with freshly peeled coconut.

This lemon marinade makes the chicken tender and moist and imparts a sweet and sour flavor.

LEMON CHICKEN

Makes 4 servings

Lemon Marinade

1/2 cup freshly squeezed lemon juice
3 tablespoons sherry
1/4 teaspoon salt
1/8 teaspoon white pepper
2 tablespoons minced parsley

2 chicken breasts, discard skin, boned, cut into 4 pieces

Peanut oil for brushing grill surface

Oriental Sauce

2 tablespoons peanut oil
2 cloves garlic, minced
3 green onions, minced
1/3 cup catsup
3 tablespoons soy sauce
1 tablespoon sesame oil
1/4 cup red wine vinegar
1/4 cup firmly packed dark brown sugar

Lemon Chicken

1/2 head iceberg lettuce
1 cup cherry tomatoes
1 lemon, sliced thinly
1/2 cup chopped parsley

To make the marinade, combine lemon juice, sherry, salt, pepper and parsley in a bowl. Pour marinade into self-sealing plastic bag. Add chicken breasts and seal the bag securely closed. Turn the bag several times, so that all areas of the chicken are coated by the marinade. Refrigerate and marinate for 1 1/2 hours. Drain, discard marinade.

Heat peanut oil in a small saucepan. Sauté garlic and onions for 3 minutes, stirring often. Add remaining ingredients and stir to combine. Continue cooking over low heat until sauce is hot. Set aside until ready to serve.

Cut lettuce in bite-sized pieces. Spread lettuce over serving plate. Sprinkle lettuce and edge the plate with cherry tomatoes. Reserve dish.

Lemon Chicken

Preheat Burton Stove Top Grill. Cut each piece of chicken into 4 strips. Brush grill surface lightly with oil. Cook chicken strips over medium-high heat for about 4 to 5 minutes. Turn once or twice during grilling. Chicken is done when it is slightly firm to the touch and juices run clear when cut with a knife. Remove chicken strips to center of prepared dish. Drizzle with heated sauce. Sprinkle with parsley. Serve hot with rice or noodles.

Black beans, sometimes called salted black beans, are purchased dried and should be washed before using. These beans can usually be found packaged in heavy plastic bags in Oriental markets. Purchase black beans that feel soft and supple through the package.

ORIENTAL CHICKEN WITH BLACK BEANS

Makes 4 servings

Soy Sauce Marinade

1/2 cup soy sauce
1/4 cup white wine
1 teaspoon sugar
1/4 teaspoon each ingredient: garlic powder, ginger powder

Oriental Black Bean Sauce

1 tablespoon fermented black beans
1 tablespoon peanut oil
2 cloves garlic, minced
3 green onions, chopped
1/2 cup chicken stock
3 tablespoons dry white wine
2 teaspoons soy sauce
1 teaspoon sugar
2 teaspoons cornstarch

Oriental Chicken With Black Beans

To make the marinade, combine soy sauce, white wine, sugar, garlic and ginger. Pour marinade into self-sealing plastic bag. Add chicken pieces and seal the bag securely closed. Turn bag several times so that all areas of the chicken are coated by the marinade. Refrigerate and marinate for 1 hour. Drain, discard marinade.

Meanwhile, prepare the Oriental black bean sauce. Rinse the black beans in a small strainer, drain. Mash beans with the back of a spoon. Heat oil in a wok or a saucepan. Fry the garlic, beans and green onions.

In a saucepan, mix in chicken stock, wine, soy sauce and sugar. Remove 1 tablespoon of sauce and mix with the cornstarch. Mix the cornstarch into the sauce. Return to saucepan. Continue simmering until sauce thickens slightly, stirring occasionally. Remove sauce from heat.

Preheat Burton Stove Top Grill. Brush chicken breasts with the sauce. Cook chicken over medium-high heat for about 5 minutes, skin side down first. Turn once during grilling. Chicken is done when it is slightly firm to the touch and juices run clear when cut with a knife. Remove chicken pieces to individual plates. Drizzle with warm sauce. Serve chicken hot. Good with white rice and grilled pineapple.

Lichees are a Chinese stone fruit, slightly larger than cherries. The flesh is white and produces an almost perfume-like taste. Canned lichees are readily available at Oriental markets.

CHICKEN WITH PINEAPPLE AND LICHEES

Makes 4 servings

Fruit Sauce

2 tablespoons peanut oil
1/2 teaspoon freshly grated ginger root
3 tablespoons soy sauce
3 tablespoons dry white wine
1/2 cup canned lichees, drained
1/2 cup canned pineapple chunks, drained
1/2 cup pineapple juice
2 tablespoons cornstarch

2 tablespoons peanut oil
1/2 teaspoon freshly grated ginger root
2 chicken breasts, discard skin, boned, cut into 4 pieces

Chicken With Pineapple and Lichee

To make sauce, heat peanut oil with ginger root in a saucepan. Stir in soy sauce and white wine. Add lichees, pineapple chunks and juice. Remove 3 tablespoons of the pineapple juice and mix with cornstarch. Blend cornstarch mixture into the sauce. Continue cooking over medium heat, stirring until the sauce thickens slightly. Set aside.

Preheat Burton Stove Top Grill. Mix oil with the freshly grated ginger root. Cut each piece of chicken into 4 or 5 strips. Brush grill surface with flavored oil. Cook chicken strips for about 4 to 5 minutes over medium-high heat, turning once or twice during grilling. Chicken is done when it is slightly firm to the touch and juices run clear when chicken strips are cut with a knife. Remove chicken strips and mound in the center of serving dish. Top with hot sauce. Serve at once. Good with rice or noodles.

CHICKEN STRIPS WITH ORANGE PLUM SAUCE

Brushing Spices

1/2 teaspoon ginger powder
1 teaspoon five spice powder
1/2 teaspoon salt
1/2 cup dry white wine

2 chicken breasts, discard skin, boned, cut into 4 pieces

Peanut oil for brushing grill surface

Orange/Plum Sauce

1/2 teaspoon freshly grated ginger root
2 teaspoons white vinegar
1 teaspoon soy sauce
4 teaspoons sugar
Freshly squeezed juice of 1 orange
1/2 cup chicken stock
2 tablespoons Grand Marnier liqueur
2 tablespoons plum sauce, available at Oriental food stores
1 tablespoon cornstarch mixed with 2 tablespoons water

1 orange, sliced, for garnish

Combine brushing spices with wine.

Cut chicken pieces into 4 or 5 strips each. Brush generously with brushing spices. Set aside and prepare sauce.

Chicken Strips With Orange Plum Sauce

Combine sauce ingredients except corn starch mixture in small sauce pan. Bring to boil over medium heat and reduce to simmer. Stir in cornstarch mixture. Simmer until the sauce thickens slightly. Reserve.

Preheat Burton Stove Top Grill. Slice each chicken piece into 4 or 5 strips. Brush grill surface lightly with oil. Cook chicken.

Cook chicken strips for about 4 to 5 minutes over medium-high heat. Turn chicken strips once or twice during grilling. Chicken is done when it is slightly firm to the touch and juices run clear when chicken strips are cut with a knife.

Remove chicken strips and mound in the center of serving dish. Top with sauce. Garnish dish with orange slices. Serve at once. Good with rice or noodles.

These burgers will be a favorite for guests on fall and winter football weekends.

Cranberry relish has a tart flavor and makes a perfect condiment with turkey. Select firm, plump berries, which can be found fresh throughout the fall and early winter.

TURKEY BURGERS WITH UNCOOKED CRANBERRY RELISH

Makes 4 servings

Uncooked Cranberry Relish

3 cups cranberries, picked over, discard any imperfect
    cranberries
2 medium apples, peeled, cored, quartered
1 orange, quartered, discard seeds
1 1/2 cups sugar
1/4 cup freshly squeezed orange juice

Makes about 3 cups

1 pound ground turkey
2 egg whites
1/4 cup finely ground whole wheat bread crumbs
1 onion, minced
1/4 teaspoon each ingredient: ground mace, salt, pepper

Turkey Burger With Uncooked Cranberry Relish

Mince cranberries, apples and orange in food processor fitted with steel blade. You may have to do it in two batches. Remove cranberry mixture to a bowl.

Stir in sugar and orange juice. Cover and refrigerate overnight. Stir and serve.

To make burgers combine ground turkey with egg whites, crumbs, onion, mace, salt and pepper. Shape into 4 patties. Place on a plate and refrigerate until ready to grill.

Preheat Burton Stove Top Grill. Cook burgers over medium-high heat, turning once. Turkey burgers will cook in about 4 minutes or grill to taste. Burgers will be crisp on the outside and cooked through on the inside. Remover burgers to individual dishes and serve hot with cranberry relish. You may want to serve on warm hamburger buns with potato salad (recipe follows).

POTATO SALAD

Makes 4 to 6 servings

1 to 1 1/4 pounds potatoes
1 red onion, chopped
1/4 cup minced parsley
2 stalks celery, chopped
3/4 cup mayonnaise
2 tablespoons each ingredient: cider vinegar, sugar
1/2 teaspoon each ingredient: salt, garlic powder
1/4 teaspoon pepper

Peel potatoes, cut into 1/2 cubes. Cover potatoes with cold water in a large saucepan. Bring to a boil over medium heat and continue cooking for 20 minutes or until the potatoes are fork tender, yet firm. Drain and cool. Cut potatoes into 1/2-inch cubes.

Place the potatoes in a bowl, toss with onion, parsley and celery. In a small dish mix together mayonnaise, vinegar, sugar, salt, garlic powder and pepper. Toss potatoes with dressing. Cover and refrigerate for 1 hour before serving.

Turkey is now available and plentiful throughout the year in supermarkets. However, you can make these turkey kabobs inside on your Burton grill even in late fall and during the holiday season when the markets are brimming with turkey and the prices are best.

Pickled peaches make a tasty and compatible side dish to this recipe.

TURKEY KABOBS WITH PICKLED PEACHES

Makes 4 servings

Pickled Peaches (recipe follows)

1 pound sliced turkey breast, about 1/2 inch thick
4 bamboo skewers, soaked in water 10 minutes, drained
8 cherry tomatoes
1/2 cup orange juice or peach juice
1 large peach, cut in quarters
1/4 cup peanut oil
1/4 teaspoon powdered ginger

Turkey Kabobs With Pickled Peaches

Cut turkey slices into 8 equal strips. Thread 1 tomato onto skewer, thread turkey, another tomato and a peach quarter. Repeat until all skewers have been threaded. Place kabobs in a glass dish. Cover with orange juice mixed with oil and ginger. Let stand 1 hour. Drain, discard marinade.

Preheat Burton Stove Top Grill. Cook turkey skewers over medium-high heat for about 5 to 6 minutes or until turkey is cooked. Turn turkey as it cooks. Turkey is done when it is slightly firm to the touch. Don't overcook turkey.

Set a kabob on each plate, spoon pickled peaches near kabob. Serve hot. Good with noodles.

Turkey Kabobs With Pickled Peaches

Pickled peaches

2 pounds ripe peaches

1/2 cup cider vinegar
1/4 cup water
3/4 cup sugar
1 tablespoon mixed pickling spices
1/2 teaspoon grated ginger
1/2 teaspoon ground cinnamon
1/2 lemon, sliced thin

Place peaches in boiling water for 1 minute. Remove peaches, discard skin and cut peaches in quarters. Reserve. Combine vinegar, water, sugar, pickling spices, ginger, mustard seeds, cinnamon and lemon slices in saucepan. Bring mixture to a boil over medium-high heat. Continue cooking for 4 to 5 minutes. Add peach quarters and cook until peaches are tender, about 10 minutes. Cool.

Spoon peaches into a glass dish, cover with syrup. Refrigerate until ready to serve.

Makes about 2 to 3 cups.

I have included this recipe as a treat to satisfy the gourmet in all of us.

GRILLED QUAIL WITH RED SEEDLESS GRAPES

Makes 4 servings

4 quail, washed, patted dry, cut in half
2 cups cornmeal
1 teaspoon lemon zest
1/4 teaspoon each ingredient: salt, freshly ground black
        pepper, dried marjoram
4 tablespoons ground almonds
Butter or margarine to brush grill surface
2 cups seedless grapes

Press quail flat. Mix together cornmeal, lemon zest, salt, pepper, marjoram and ground almonds. Spread mixture on flat plate. Roll quail in the flavored cornmeal.

Preheat Burton Stove Top Grill. Brush grill surface with butter. Cook quail over medium-high heat for 2 to 3 minutes per side or until done to taste.

Quail will be crispy on the outside and tender on the inside. Quail are cooked when juices run clear when pricked with a fork. Do not overcook. Remove each quail to a dish, sprinkle with grapes. Serve quail hot. Good with grilled polenta or grilled zucchini.

SEAFOOD

Seafood provides nearly the perfect combination of taste and nutritional value. Most fish have very low levels of fat and a high protein content. Fish serve as an excellent entrée for low cholesterol diets, weight-reduction diets, and low sodium diets. Most fish dishes are delicate and sweet-tasting.

In some recipes in this chapter, I have used the Grill Lid with the Burton grill. This allows thicker cuts of fish, for instance fish steaks, to cook more thoroughly and delicately. Fish cooking demands care and observation. Many fish dishes are overcooked, which totally corrupts the entire concept of fish cookery. Over-cooked fish becomes dry and tasteless. Shrimp and other shellfish become rubbery and unpleasant when over-cooked.

If you are a fisherman, dress and chill your catch as quickly as you can, preferably straight from the water. Grill a fresh catch the same day, if possible. You can freeze your catch, but it is best to thaw and grill it within as short a time period as you can.

In this chapter, enjoy recipes from Grilled Rainbow Trout with Parsley and Lemon, to Crusted Bluefish with Grilled Endive, to Shrimp Enchiladas.

Cut salmon steaks into strips for grilling.

Mint is a pungent, aromatic herb which grows wild throughout the world and is very commonly found in herb gardens or as a border plant. You can generally find fresh mint in the supermarket throughout the year.

SALMON STRIPS WITH CHOPPED MINT AND TOMATOES

Makes 4 servings

Chopped Mint and Tomatoes

4 large ripe tomatoes
1 cup mint leaves
1/4 cup minced cilantro
3 green onions, minced
1/4 cup extra virgin olive oil
1/4 cup freshly squeezed lemon juice
1/4 teaspoon each ingredient: salt, pepper, garlic powder

2 tablespoons extra virgin olive oil
1 teaspoon minced mint
1/4 teaspoon pepper
4 salmon fillets, about 6 ounces each

Cut tomatoes in half. Squeeze tomatoes to discard seeds. Chop tomatoes and place in bowl. Mince mint and toss with tomatoes. Blend in cilantro, onions, olive oil, lemon juice, salt, pepper and garlic powder. Allow sauce to marinate for 30 minutes at room temperature. Toss before serving. Taste to adjust seasonings.

Salmon Strips With Chopped Mint And Tomatoes

To prepare salmon strips, mix the oil with mint and pepper. Cut salmon into 1 inch strips. Brush salmon with flavored oil.

Preheat Burton Stove Top Grill. Cook salmon strips over medium-high heat for about 4 to 5 minutes. Grill each side for about 2 minutes. Salmon is cooked when it flakes easily when prodded with a fork.

Remove salmon strips to a platter and serve immediately with chopped mint and tomatoes. Good with pasta.

GRILLED SALMON

Makes 4 servings

4 salmon fillets, about 6 ounces each
2 tablespoons peanut oil

Brush salmon fillets with oil.

Preheat Burton Stove Top Grill. Cook fillets over medium-high heat for about 2 to 3 minutes on each side or until fish is done to taste. Fish is done when it flakes easily when prodded with a fork. Remove salmon fillets to individual dinner plates. Serve immediately.

Swordfish is dense and meaty and is usually sold as steaks. Use the Grill Lid for this recipe.

Tarragon goes very well with fish dishes. It is nice if you can use fresh tarragon. As it is an herb widely used in French cooking, French chefs grow tarragon year round in their herb gardens. Start an indoor herb garden, and it will reward you with fresh herbs throughout the year.

SWORDFISH WITH CHIVE SAUCE

Chive Sauce

1/2 teaspoon dry mustard
1 1/2 tablespoons freshly grated ginger
1 egg yolk
2 shallots, peeled
1/4 teaspoon white pepper
2 teaspoons soy sauce
1/4 cup chopped chives
2 cloves garlic, peeled
Freshly squeezed juice of 1 lemon
3/4 cup extra virgin olive oil

To prepare sauce, use a food processor fitted with steel blade.

Blend mustard, ginger, egg yolk, shallots, pepper, soy sauce, chives, garlic and lemon juice. With the machine running, drizzle olive oil into the bowl until all olive oil has been added and the sauce is well blended. Pour sauce into a bowl, cover and refrigerate until ready to serve.

Swordfish With Chive Sauce

Stir before serving and serve at room temperature.

4 swordfish steaks, about 6 ounces each
2 tablespoons extra virgin olive oil

Brush swordfish steaks with olive oil.

Preheat Burton Stove Top Grill. Cook swordfish over medium-high heat for 2 to 3 minutes on each side or until done. Swordfish is done when it becomes lightly firm to the touch and flakes easily when prodded with a fork. Do not overcook as fish will be tough. You can cover with the Grill Lid the last 3 or 4 minutes if desired. Remove to serving dish. Spoon sauce onto 4 dinner plates. Set a piece of swordfish on the sauce. Serve hot. Good with pineapple cole slaw (recipe follows).

PINEAPPLE COLE SLAW

Makes 6 servings

6 cups shredded cabbage
1 onion, sliced thinly
1 large carrot, grated
1 cup crushed pineapple, drained

Dressing

1/2 to 3/4 cup mayonnaise
2 tablespoons sugar
2 tablespoons cider vinegar
3/4 teaspoon salt
1/2 teaspoon garlic powder
1/4 teaspoon white pepper

Place shredded cabbage in deep bowl. Toss cabbage with onion, carrot and pineapple. Mix mayonnaise, sugar, vinegar, salt, garlic powder and pepper. Pour dressing over vegetables and toss well. Refrigerate overnight. Taste to adjust seasonings. Toss and serve.

This recipe, unlike most of the fish recipes included here, is quite rich. It makes a wonderful dish to serve to company.

Raspberries are considered by many to be the most elegant of all berries. The peak season for raspberries is July in most areas, but they can be found from early summer to November. Raspberries are highly perishable and should be used as soon as possible after they are purchased.

TUNA WITH RASPBERRY SAUCE

Makes 4 servings

Processor Raspberry Sauce

1 package, 10 ounces, frozen raspberries, defrosted,
    juice included
1/2 cup sugar
2 eggs
1 egg yolk
2 tablespoons raspberry vinegar
1/4 teaspoon each ingredient: dried basil, pepper
1/2 teaspoon dried tarragon
2 cups extra virgin olive oil

4 tuna fillets, about 6 ounces each
2 tablespoons extra virgin olive oil
1/2 teaspoon dried tarragon

Tuna With Raspberry Sauce

To prepare raspberry sauce, fit a food processor with a steel blade, purée raspberries with the juice. Spoon raspberry purée into a saucepan. Stir in sugar and simmer for 10 minutes. Strain and cool.

Again, using the food processor, whip the eggs and egg yolk about 20 seconds. Remove the top of the processor and add vinegar, basil, pepper and tarragon. Blend for 1 minute. Add raspberry mixture and again process for 1 minute. With the machine running, drizzle in the oil until all the oil has been added and sauce is well blended. Pour sauce into a bowl, cover and refrigerate until serving time.

Mix oil with tarragon. Brush tuna fillets with flavored oil. Preheat Burton Stove Top Grill. Cook tuna fillets over medium-high heat, about 1 minute on each side. Cover tuna on grill with the Grill Lid and continue cooking for 2 to 3 minutes or until fish is done. Fish is cooked when it flakes easily when prodded with the fork.

Remove fish and place on individual plates, drizzle with sauce. Pass sauce at the table. Good with fettucine.

Grouper slices into excellent fillets. The meat is lean and firm and makes super sandwiches.

Horseradish can often be obtained fresh and grated for use in many dishes. However, for this recipe, use a mild bottled horseradish sauce. Horseradish is spicy and pungent and makes a wonderful sauce for this delicious sandwich.

GROUPER SANDWICH WITH HORSERADISH SAUCE

Makes 4 servings

Onion Marinade

1 tablespoon peanut oil
1 medium onion, minced
1/2 cup beer
3 tablespoons cider vinegar
1/2 teaspoon dry mustard
1/4 teaspoon each ingredient: pepper, ground cumin

Heat oil in saucepan. Sauté onion for 4 minutes over medium heat, stirring occasionally. Stir in remaining ingredients. Cool marinade.

Pour marinade into self-sealing plastic bag. Slice in grouper and seal the bag securely closed. Turn bag several times, so that all surfaces of the fish are coated by the marinade. Refrigerate and marinate for 2 hours, turning several times. Remove fish from marinade, discard marinade.

Grouper Sandwich With Horseradish Sauce

2 tablespoons white horseradish
1 cup low-fat, plain yogurt

2 tablespoons peanut oil
4 grouper fillets, about 6 ounces each
4 burger rolls, sliced, warmed on the grill
4 lettuce leaves
4 large slices tomato
4 slices onion, optional

Set a roll on each plate. Place a lettuce leaf on the open roll. Mix horseradish with yogurt, and put it in a bowl.

Preheat Burton Stove Top Grill. Brush grill surface lightly with peanut oil and grill grouper fillets over medium-high heat, about 2 minutes on each side or until fish is done to taste. Fish will flake easily when done.

Remove grouper and set on lettuce. Top with tomato. Pass horseradish sauce at table. Good with chopped pickles.

ORANGE ROUGHY WITH SPROUT RELISH

Makes 4 servings

Sprout relish

1/2 pound bean sprouts
4 stalks celery, minced
1 small onion, minced
1 red bell pepper, chopped
1/2 cup chopped olives
1/4 cup cider vinegar
3/4 cup sugar
2 teaspoons salt
1/4 teaspoon pepper

Peanut oil for brushing grill surface
1 1/4 pounds orange roughy fillets, cut into 4 pieces

Toss sprouts, celery, onion, pepper, olives, vinegar, sugar, salt and pepper in a deep bowl. Cover and marinate in refrigerator the day before serving. Taste to adjust seasonings, and toss before serving.

Makes about 1 1/2 cups.

Orange Roughy With Sprout Relish

Preheat Burton Stove Top Grill. Brush grill surface lightly with peanut oil. Cook fish fillets over medium-high heat, 2 minutes per side or until done. Fish will flake easily when prodded with a fork and the color of fish will become opaque.

Remove each serving to individual plates; serve with sprout relish.

ORANGE ROUGHY WITH CHILI SAUCE

Makes 4 servings

Chili Sauce

1 1/2 cups low-fat, plain yogurt
3 tablespoons chili sauce
3 green onions, minced

1/4 teaspoon each ingredient: ground thyme, chili powder
1 1/4 to 1 1/2 pounds orange roughy
2 tablespoons butter or margarine, melted

1 medium red onion cut into 4 thin slices

To prepare chili sauce, combine yogurt, chili paste and chopped green onion in a small bowl. Cover and refrigerate until serving time. Stir before serving.

Mix thyme and barbecue powder into melted butter. Brush fish with flavored butter.

Preheat Burton Stove Top Grill. Grill orange roughy pieces, over medium heat on both sides until fish is cooked. Fish is best when lightly cooked. Do not overcook. Fish will become opaque and slightly firm to touch. Remove roughy to individual plates. Spoon chili sauce over center of fish. Serve immediately.

Sweet potato pie is a popular dish in the South and deserves a wider recognition and enjoyment. It is superb as either a side dish or as a dessert.

CATFISH WITH SWEET POTATO PIE

Makes 4 servings

Sweet potato pie (recipe follows)

1 cup evaporated milk
2 cups white cornmeal
1/2 teaspoon paprika
1/4 teaspoon each ingredient: dried sage, dried thyme, pepper
4 catfish fillets, about 6 ounces each

Peanut oil for brushing grill surface

Pour evaporated milk into a shallow bowl.

Mix together cornmeal, paprika, sage, thyme and pepper. Spread on a flat plate. Dip fish in milk. Drain. Roll catfish fillets in cornmeal mixture. Set catfish on a plate and refrigerate until serving time.

Preheat Burton Stove Top Grill. Brush grill surface lightly with peanut oil. Cook catfish over medium high heat for about 4 minutes, turning once or twice until done. Fish is cooked when it flakes easily when prodded with a fork.

Remove fish and set on individual plates. Serve with generous portion of sweet potato pie and salad.

SWEET POTATO PIE

Makes 4 to 6 servings

3 cups cooked sweet potatoes, puréed
1/4 teaspoon each ingredient: ground nutmeg, ground allspice,
     salt
1/2 teaspoon ground cinnamon
1 cup firmly packed light brown sugar
3 eggs, lightly beaten
1/2 pint half-and-half
4 tablespoons butter or margarine, melted
1 unbaked 9 inch pie crust

Preheat oven to 450 degrees F.

Place puréed sweet potatoes in a large deep mixing bowl. Blend
nutmeg, allspice, salt, cinnamon, sugar and eggs. Blend in half-
and-half and butter.

Spoon sweet potato filling into prepared crust; smooth filling out to
reach edges of crust with the back of a spoon.

Bake the pie for 10 minutes. Reduce heat to 250 degrees F and
continue baking for 20 minutes or until a pie tester inserted in the
center of the pie comes out clean.

Serve sweet potato pie hot or cold.

The trout is stuffed with parsley sprigs and lemon slices which keep the fish moist and impart a delightful flavor.

GRILLED RAINBOW TROUT
WITH PARSLEY AND LEMON BUTTER

Makes 2 servings

Parsley and Lemon Butter

4 tablespoons butter or margarine, room temperature
4 1/4 cups minced parsley
1 teaspoon lemon zest

2 rainbow trout, about 8 ounces each
4 sprigs parsley
1 lemon, sliced thinly
2 tablespoons margarine or butter, melted

1 tablespoon peanut oil
1/4 teaspoon each ingredient: salt, pepper, garlic powder, dried thyme

To make parsley and lemon butter, soften butter in a bowl with the back of a spoon or use a food processor fitted with steel blade. Mix in parsley and lemon zest. Spoon flavored butter into a small bowl or crock. Cover and set aside. Serve at room temperature.

Grilled Rainbow Trout With Parsley And Lemon Butter

Wash trout and pat dry with paper towels. Combine butter, oil, salt, pepper, garlic powder and thyme. Brush fish with seasoned butter. Slide lemon slices and sprigs of parsley into the cavity of the fish.

Preheat Burton Stove Top Grill. Cook trout over medium-high heat for about 1 minute on each side. Cover with the Grill Lid. Turn trout and continue grilling, covered, until fish is cooked, about 2 minutes longer. When done, fish will flake easily when prodded with a fork.

Place 1 trout on each plate; serve with parsley and lemon butter garnish and lemon slices. Good with salad and lemon blueberry muffins (recipe follows).

If batter doesn't fill all the muffin cups, fill the empty cups with 1 inch of water to protect the pan during baking.

LEMON BLUEBERRY MUFFINS

Makes 10 to 12 muffins

2 cups blueberries, picked over or defrosted blueberries
6 tablespoons margarine or butter, room temperature
1 cup sugar
2 eggs
1 cup low-fat, plain yogurt or sour cream
2 cups unbleached all-purpose flour
1 teaspoon baking powder
1 teaspoon baking soda
1/2 teaspoon salt
1 teaspoon each ingredient: lemon juice, ground cinnamon, lemon zest

Preheat oven to 350 degrees F.

Wash and drain blueberries; pat dry on paper towels.

Grease muffin tins, 12 (2 1/2 inch) muffin cups, or use paper liners.

Blend together butter, sugar, eggs and yogurt in electric mixer. Blend in flour, baking powder, baking soda, salt, lemon juice and cinnamon. Slowly stir in blueberries using a spoon.

Lemon Blueberry Muffins

Fill muffin cups 2/3 full. Wipe off any spilled drips. Bake muffins 30 to 35 minutes or until golden brown on top and tests dry with a baking tester. Loosen muffins with spatula and set on a wire rack to cool.

I have included a recipe for blackening seasoning. Be sure to open your windows while grilling this recipe.

Red beans and rice is another New Orleans favorite that can be served alone as an entrée or as a side dish with many foods.

BLACKENED REDFISH

Makes 4 servings

Blackening Spices

1 tablespoon dried minced onion
1 1/2 teaspoons cayenne
1/2 teaspoon each ingredient: garlic powder, dried thyme, celery salt, salt
1/4 teaspoon pepper
4 tablespoons butter or margarine, melted
4 redfish fillets, about 6 ounces each
1 tablespoon peanut oil

Combine onion, cayenne, garlic powder, dried thyme, celery salt, salt and pepper. Mix melted butter and peanut oil with blackening spices. Place blackening mixture into a shallow bowl.

Pat fish dry with paper towels. Roll each fish fillet in the blackening mixture. Set fish on a plate and refrigerate until ready to grill.

Blackened Redfish

Preheat Burton Stove Top Grill. Cook fish over high heat for about 2 minutes. Make sure your kitchen is well ventilated; open a window. Turn fish over, cover with the grill lid and continue cooking over medium-high heat for 2 to 3 minutes longer or until fish is cooked. Fish will blacken slightly on the outside and be opaque on the inside.

Remove to serving plate. Serve with coleslaw, red beans and rice (recipe follows).

RED BEANS AND RICE

Makes 6 to 8 servings

1 pound red beans, soaked in water overnight, drained, reserve water
1 large onion, diced
1 carrot sliced thinly
1/2 teaspoon salt
2 bay leaves
1 ham bone
2 tablespoons peanut oil
3 stalks celery, sliced thinly
1/2 teaspoon hot pepper sauce
1/2 teaspoon salt
1/4 teaspoon cayenne
1 cup long grain rice
3 tablespoons peanut oil
3/4 teaspoon salt

Cover beans with reserved liquid and enough additional water to measure 6 cups liquid in a large pan. Add half of the onion and the carrot, salt, bay leaves and ham bone. Cover beans and simmer for 2 1/2 to 3 hours, stir occasionally.

Heat oil in a frying pan. Sauté celery and the remaining onion until tender, stirring occasionally about 5 minutes. Remove the ham bone from beans. Separate off any ham from the bone. Stir ham and vegetables into the beans.

Remove 1 cup of the beans; purée it and return it to the pot. Add seasonings; keep warm. Discard bay leaves.

Red Beans And Rice

Place rice and 2 cups of water, oil and salt in a saucepan. Cover and cook over medium heat for 15 to 20 minutes.

To serve, place a scoop of rice in a shallow bowl. Ladle beans over rice. Serve hot.

FLOUNDER WITH ANISE MARINADE

Makes 4 servings

Anise Marinade

1/2 cup dry white wine
1/4 cup extra virgin olive oil
1/4 teaspoon anise seeds
3 tablespoons minced parsley

4 flounder fillets, about 6 ounces each

Combine white wine, olive oil, anise seeds and parsley. Pour marinade into self-sealing plastic bag. Add flounder fillets and seal the bag securely closed. Turn bag several times so that all surfaces of fish are coated by the marinade. Refrigerate and marinate for 1 hour, turning once. Drain, discard marinade.

Preheat Burton Stove Top Grill. Cook flounder over medium-high heat about 4 to 5 minutes, turning once. Remove flounder to serving dish. Serve hot. Good with warm garlic bread.

Endive, a member of the chicory family, has tightly packed white or pale yellow leaves. While slightly bitter, this vegetable is marvelous grilled. Cut the endives into two length-wise pieces to grill.

CRUSTED BLUEFISH WITH GRILLED ENDIVE

Makes 4 servings

Cornmeal Coating

2 cups white cornmeal
3 tablespoons minced parsley
1/2 teaspoon dried rosemary
1/4 teaspoon dried thyme

4 bluefish fillets, about 6 ounces each
Peanut oil for brushing grill

2 tablespoons peanut oil
1/4 teaspoon dried thyme
2 heads endive, blanched, drained

To prepare cornmeal coating, mix cornmeal, parsley, rosemary and thyme. Spread mixture evenly onto a flat plate.

Roll bluefish fillets in cornmeal coating. Set fillets on a dish and refrigerate until ready to grill.

Crusted Bluefish With Grilled Endive

Preheat Burton Stove Top Grill. Brush grill surface lightly with oil. Grill bluefish fillets over medium-high heat about 5 minutes, turning once or twice. Fish is done when it flakes easily when prodded with a fork. For best results, do not overcook. Remove fish to platter.

Mix peanut oil with thyme. Brush endive with flavored oil. Grill endive, cut side down, about 1 1/2 minutes. Endive will be a golden brown. Turn once and grill a minute or longer to taste. Put endive on serving dish around bluefish, serve at once. Good with a tossed salad.

Whitefish, a member of the salmon and trout family, is common to the Great Lakes and other cold, deep fresh waters. It is available throughout the country.

WHITEFISH WITH GRILLED GREEN ONIONS

Makes 4 servings

Tabasco Marinade

1/2 cup peanut oil
3 tablespoons freshly squeezed lime juice
1/4 teaspoon Tabasco sauce

4 whitefish fillets, about 6 ounces each

8 green onions, trimmed

Combine oil, lime juice and Tabasco sauce. Pour marinade into self-sealing plastic bag. Add fish and green onions. Seal the bag securely closed. Turn bag several times so that all surfaces of fish and onions are coated by the marinade. Refrigerate and marinate for 1 hour, turning once. Drain whitefish. Separate onions.

Preheat Burton Stove Top Grill. Cook whitefish over medium-high heat about 4 to 5 minutes, turning once. Remove each piece to an individual dish. Grill onions, 1 minute on each side. Arrange 2 onions on each piece of whitefish. Serve hot. Good with lime wedges and spinach salad.

REDFISH WITH RED WINE SAUCE

Makes 4 servings

Red Wine Sauce

2 large shallots, minced
1 cup red wine
2 tablespoons half and half
8 tablespoons unsalted butter, cut into 1/2 inch chunks
1/4 teaspoon each ingredient: salt, white pepper, dried
      tarragon

4 fillets redfish, about 6 ounces each
2 tablespoons peanut oil
1/4 cup minced chives, for garnish

To prepare sauce, cook the shallots and red wine in a small saucepan over medium heat until liquid has been reduced to about 3 to 4 tablespoons. Strain and return the liquid to a saucepan. Blend in the cream and continue cooking over low heat until warm. Whisk in the butter, a few chunks at a time. Season with salt, pepper and tarragon.

Brush redfish fillets with peanut oil.

Redfish With Red Wine Sauce

Preheat Burton Stove Top Grill. Cook fillets over medium-high heat about 2 minutes per side, turning once, or until fish is cooked. Fish is done when it flakes easily when prodded with a fork, and fish is opaque.

Spoon sauce onto a heated plate, set redfish on top of sauce. Garnish top of fish with minced chives.

Taramasalata is a Greek sauce made from a base of tarama, which is cod roe. You can purchase 4 ounce jars of tarama in Greek markets or specialty food stores. In this recipe, half of the tarmasalata is used as a sauce for the cod fillets; the remaining portion is used as a dip with crusty bread chunks.

COD WITH TARAMASALATA

Makes 4 servings

Taramasalata

3 thin slices white bread, crust removed, torn into quarters
1 small onion, quartered
1 jar, 4 ounces, tarama, available at large super markets or at a Greek market

2 small cloves garlic
3 tablespoons freshly squeezed lemon juice
1/2 cup extra virgin olive oil

Place bread in the food processor and make into crumbs. Add remaining ingredients except olive oil. Purée tarama mixture. With the machine running, add olive oil in a slow steady stream. Mixture must be smooth and almost a light pink in color. Spoon into a crock or bowl, taste to adjust seasonings, cover and refrigerate until serving time.

Cod With Taramasalata

2 tablespoons extra virgin olive oil
1 teaspoon freshly squeezed lemon juice
4 cod steaks or fillets, about 6 ounces each

Mix together olive oil and juice. Brush cod fillets.

Preheat Burton Stove Top Grill. Cook cod fillets over medium-high heat about 5 minutes or until done, turning fish once.

Cod is cooked when it flakes easily when prodded with a fork. Remove fish cod fillets to serving dish.

Spoon taramasalata sauce on fish. Serve French bread (cut into thin slices) dipped in remaining taramasalata, as a side dish to the cod fillets.

Kippers are actually herring which are split from head to tail, lightly brined, and then cold smoked. Wash before grilling. The grilling process here is used merely to warm the kippers. Do not overcook them.

GRILLED KIPPERS

Makes 2 servings

3 tablespoons butter or margarine, melted
1 tablespoon peanut oil
1/4 teaspoon pepper
2 slices red onion, 1/2 inch thick
1 green bell pepper, seeded, sliced into 1/2 inch rounds

2 smoked kippers, available at large fish stores

Combine melted butter, oil and pepper. Brush onion and pepper slices with margarine mixture.

Brush kippers with butter mixture.

Preheat Burton Stove Top Grill. Cook onion and pepper slices over medium heat for about 1 minute on each side. Vegetables will begin to brown and be warm. Remove vegetables to a dish.

Grill smoked kippers over medium heat about 2 minutes on each side, covered with Grill Lid. Remember kippers have been smoked commercially. We are only heating them, so do not overcook.

Remove kippers and place 1 kipper on each plate. Put an onion slice and pepper rings on each kipper. Serve hot.

SEA SCALLOPS WITH TOMATO AND TARRAGON

Makes 4 servings

Tomato and Tarragon

2 large, ripe tomatoes
2 tablespoons extra virgin olive oil
2 teaspoons freshly squeezed lemon juice
3 tablespoons fresh, minced tarragon
Salt and pepper to taste

2 tablespoons butter or margarine, melted
1 tablespoon extra virgin olive oil
1/4 teaspoonful pepper
1 1/4 pounds sea scallops with roe, if possible

To make sauce, cut tomatoes, squeeze out seeds and chop. Place tomatoes in a colander and drain for 5 minutes. Put chopped tomatoes in a bowl. Mix in olive oil, lemon juice, 1 tablespoon tarragon, salt and pepper to taste. Cover tightly and refrigerate until serving time. Just before serving, toss tomato and tarragon. Taste to adjust seasonings. Spoon chopped tomatoes onto plate.

Combine melted butter with oil and pepper. Brush scallops with flavored butter.

Sprinkle remaining tarragon in the water pan. Replace grill surface. Preheat Burton Stove Top Grill. Cook scallops over medium-high heat about 2 minutes on each side. Remove scallops from grill and set over tomato sauce. Serve hot. Good with sliced cucumber and pasta shells.

Tomatillos are small, green tomato-like fruits which are cooked with the skin intact. They can be found in specialty food stores or in Latin American markets. Tomatillos have a very interesting flavor which hints of lemon, apples and herbs.

SHRIMP ENCHILADAS

Makes 6 servings

Sauce

3 tablespoons peanut oil
2 cloves garlic, minced
1/2 teaspoon salt
3 green onions, minced
2 cans, 10 ounces each, tomatillos, puréed with juice
2 to 3 jalapeno peppers, seeded, chopped, using rubber
      gloves
3/4 teaspoon ground cumin
1/2 teaspoon ground oregano
2 corn tortillas, crumbled

1 large onion, sliced into 6 slices
Peanut oil for brushing grill
1/2 teaspoon ground cumin
1 1/2 cups large shrimp, deveined, washed
6 flour or corn tortillas

1 cup low-fat plain yogurt
Grilled avocado slices

233

Shrimp Enchiladas

Heat the oil in saucepan over medium heat. Sauté garlic, salt and onions, for 4 minutes, stirring often. Mix in peppers, tomatillos, cumin and oregano. Add tortillas. Simmer 4 to 5 minutes. Cool sauce. Purée in food processor fitted with steel blade or use a blender. Set aside.

Mix oil with cumin. Brush shrimp with flavored oil.

Preheat Burton Stove Top Grill. Cook shrimp over medium-high heat, about 3 minutes, turning once. Shrimp will turn opaque and become slightly firm. Do not overcook as they become tough. Reserve.

Warm tortillas, one at a time, just a few seconds on each side on the grill. Turn tortillas once.

Grill onion slices, 1 minute per side. Remove from grill and set aside.

Preheat oven to 400 degrees F.

Arrange 1/4 cup of the grilled shrimp in the center of each tortilla. Place 1 slice of onion over shrimp. Top with 2 to 3 tablespoons of sauce.

Shrimp Enchiladas

Roll up the tortilla and set into a flat casserole dish. Cover tortillas with remaining sauce.

Bake 10 minutes. Tortillas should be hot. Serve hot with yogurt and avocado slices. Good with refried beans, sliced olives and grated cheddar cheese.

Soft-shell crabs are blue crabs which have moulted their hard shells in order to grow a new, larger shell. They should be eaten on the day they are purchased. The entire soft-shell crab is edible, so encourage your guests to eat the entire crab.

BREADED SOFT-SHELLED CRABS

Makes 4 servings

Breading

2 cups fine bread crumbs
1/2 teaspoon each ingredient: dried oregano, dried basil
1 tablespoon minced parsley
1/4 teaspoon salt
1/8 teaspoon pepper

2 tablespoons butter or margarine, melted
2 tablespoons extra virgin olive oil
8 soft-shelled crabs

Breading

To prepare breading, mix bread crumbs with oregano, basil, parsley, salt and pepper. Spread on a flat dish. Set aside.

Combine melted butter and olive oil and pour into a shallow bowl. Reserve.

Breaded Soft-Shelled Crabs

To clean the soft-shell crabs, do 1 crab at a time and place it on a cutting board. Remove the face portion of the crab. Lift the shell, it lifts easily, on either side of the back. Scrape off the gills. Lift the shell, and then remove the sand holder from under the face area. Throw away all sections that you remove from the crab. Then wash the shelled crab and dry it. Continue until all the soft-shell crabs have been cleaned. It is always a better idea to have the capable person at the fish counter clean the crabs for you. They do it very quickly and efficiently.

Roll crabs in melted butter and then dust crab generously in the bread crumbs, patting crumbs to stick securely onto the melted butter.

Preheat Burton Stove Top Grill. Cook crabs over medium-high heat for about 4 to 5 minutes, turning once. Crabs are cooked when they change color. They change from a bluish hue to a slightly reddish color, and they become slightly firm to the touch. Serve with your favorite potato dish and a salad. Serve 2 crabs to a guest and eat the complete crab.

I have included this recipe as a fun and clever presentation for guests. You will need to use the Grill Lid with the Burton grill. Buy mussels which have tightly closed shells. Thoroughly scrub the mussel shells before grilling. Wrap five mussels in a packet of foil and add a bit of white wine and garlic. Make an individual packet for each guest. Steam the packets on the Burton grill, and serve each guest his own mussel packet. Eat only mussels that have opened their shells during steaming.

MUSSEL PACKETS

Makes 4 servings

20 mussels

Aluminum foil

1/4 cup dry, white wine
2 garlic cloves, minced
1 medium onion, minced
1 medium tomato, sliced thinly

Wash mussels, discard any opened mussels.

Cut 4 double thickness of aluminum foil, large enough to hold 5 mussels in a packet. Set the foil out flat. Place mussels in the center of the foil. Sprinkle with white wine, garlic, onion and tomato slices.

Wrap the foil around the mussels and twist shut.

Mussel Packets

Preheat Burton Stove Top Grill. Set mussel packet on grill surface over high heat. Cover packets with the Grill Lid. Cook for 4 to 5 minutes or until mussels open.

Place a mussel packet on each plate. Allow guests to open their own packet. Tell guests to discard any mussels that have not opened. Serve hot. Good with salad and garlic bread.

TROUT WITH ALMONDS

Makes 4 servings

4 trout fillets
2 tablespoons extra virgin olive oil
Salt and pepper to taste
1/2 cup chopped almonds

Brush trout fillets with oil and sprinkle with salt and pepper.

Preheat Burton Stove Top Grill. Cook trout over medium heat, turning once. Fish is done when it flakes easily when prodded with a fork. Place fish on individual dinner plates and sprinkle with almonds. Serve hot.

VEGETABLES

Vegetables are probably far more abused in cooking than is meat. Ideally, vegetables should be picked fresh from the garden, cooked immediately after picking, and cooked to precision. Too often vegetables are cooked to death, far beyond their ability to retain their natural flavors and textures. While the Burton Stove Top Grill was not designed solely to facilitate the correct cooking of vegetables, it does work masterfully with vegetable dishes. The intense heat cooks virtually any vegetable quickly and thoroughly, while allowing the vegetable to retain both flavor and the desired degree of crunchiness.

Thick vegetables, such as potatoes, carrots and whole onions, should be sliced for the most effective cooking on the Burton grill. If thick vegetables are desired, they should be boiled or blanched before being used on the grill. However, as always, they should not be over-cooked. The grill will help to revive the texture of pre-cooked vegetables.

During the summer and fall, always use the fresh bounty of the garden. During winter and early spring, you can enjoy the thrill of the grill with frozen vegetables and fill your kitchen and heart with the aroma of grilling vegetables while the snow is falling outside.

Recipes from Artichoke and Mushroom Kabobs, to Grilled Eggplant Slices with Parsley, to Corn-on-the-Cob with Blue Cheese Butter are included in this chapter.

This is a unique and tangy approach to corn on the cob. The sweetest and freshest flavor of corn is obtained by using corn immediately after picking. If you are buying corn from a vegetable stand or at a farmer's market, ask for corn that has been picked that day.

I am a blue cheese fanatic. I think blue cheese works extremely well with virtually any food. Blue cheese has a bite and flavor that adds zest to a dish.

CORN ON THE COB
WITH BLUE CHEESE BUTTER

Makes 4 servings

4 fresh ears of corn

Blue cheese butter

4 tablespoons butter or margarine, room temperature
3 ounces crumbled blue cheese
1/4 teaspoon Dijon mustard

Bend back husks from the corn. Remove silk from corn. Replace outer husks. Soak corn in the husk, covered in water for 10 minutes, drain.

Corn On The Cob With Blue Cheese Butter

Meanwhile, prepare blue cheese butter. Soften butter in a bowl, using the back of a spoon or use a food processor fitted with steel blade. Mix in blue cheese and Dijon mustard. Spoon the flavored butter into a bowl or crock.

Again pull back outer husks, brush corn liberally with blue cheese butter.

Preheat Burton Stove Top Grill. Grill corn over medium heat, about 3 minutes, rotating after each minute. Corn husks will char slightly, but corn will be tender and warm. Remove to serving dish, serve hot. You may want to serve extra blue cheese butter with the hot corn.

Eggplants are available in most produce departments throughout the year, although they are most plentiful in the late summer and early fall. Eggplants retain a good deal of moisture; to remove excess moisture, salt and drain eggplant slices on a rack before grilling. Eggplant discolors rapidly, but will retain a fresh look if sprinkled with lemon juice. Choose eggplants that are firm and heavy, with a dark, shiny, smooth skin.

Parmesan is an Italian hard cheese which imparts a strong, fragrant quality to this dish.

EGGPLANT PARMIGIANA ON THE GRILL

Makes 4 servings

1 medium eggplant, peeled, cut into 1/2 inch slices
Salt
1/2 teaspoon dried oregano
Extra virgin olive oil for brushing eggplant slices
8 tablespoons tomato sauce
4 slices mozzarella cheese, slightly smaller than each eggplant
     slice
1/4 cup freshly grated Parmesan cheese
1 tablespoon minced parsley

Spread eggplant slices on paper towels. Sprinkle with salt and let stand for 40 minutes. Wash off salt, pat eggplant dry with paper towels.

Preheat Burton Stove Top Grill. Mix oregano with olive oil. Brush eggplant slices with flavored oil. Grill eggplant over medium-high heat for 1 1/2 to 2 minutes per side.

Eggplant Parmigiana On The Grill

While eggplant is still on the grill, spread 2 tablespoons tomato sauce on each eggplant slice, using the back of a spoon to spread the tomato sauce. Layer a slice of mozzarella cheese on each eggplant slice. Sprinkle with Parmesan cheese. Continue grilling another 1 to 2 minutes. Mozzarella cheese will begin to melt around edges, and eggplant will be cooked through.

Remove eggplant slices to serving dish. Sprinkle with parsley and serve immediately.

GRILLED EGGPLANT SLICES WITH PARSLEY SAUCE

Makes 4 servings

1 eggplant, cut into 1/2 inch slices
Salt

Parsley Sauce

2 tablespoons freshly squeezed lemon juice
2 cloves garlic, minced
3 anchovy fillets, drained
1/4 cup chopped parsley
2 teaspoons capers
1 small boiled potato, peeled, cut in half
1/4 teaspoon pepper

1/4 cup extra virgin olive oil
3 tablespoons extra virgin olive oil
1/2 teaspoon dried oregano

Spread the eggplant slices on paper towels, sprinkle with salt. Let eggplant slices stand for 40 minutes. Wash off salt, pat dry with paper towels.

While eggplant slices are draining, prepare parsley sauce. Using a food processor fitted with steel blade, puree all sauce ingredients. With the machine running, pour 1/4 cup oil through the food tube until ingredients are blended. Pour sauce into a bowl, cover and refrigerate.

Grilled Eggplant Slices With Parsley Sauce

Mix 3 tablespoons olive oil with dried oregano. Brush eggplant slices with flavored oil.

Preheat Burton Stove Top Grill. Cook eggplant slices over medium-high heat about 2 minutes on each side. Eggplant will be a golden brown on the outside and tender on the inside. Remove eggplant slices to serving dish. Drizzle with parsley sauce. Serve hot.

Avocados are native to America and are absolutely rich in vitamins. While avocados are best known as the soul of guacamole, these grilled avocado slices make a delicious and creative addition to a meal.

AVOCADO SLICES

Makes 4 servings

1 large ripe avocado
3 tablespoons freshly squeezed lime juice

Butter or margarine to brush avocado
4 lettuce leaves

1 can, 4 ounces, mild green chilies, drained, seeded
2 tablespoons minced cilantro

Peel avocado, discard pit, and slice. Sprinkle avocado with lime juice.

Preheat Burton Stove Top Grill. Brush avocado slices with butter. Grill avocado slices over medium-high heat for 1 minute per side. Avocado will be warm on the inside and lightly browned on the outside.

Arrange a lettuce leaf on each salad plate. Arrange avocado slices over lettuce. Sprinkle with chilies and minced cilantro. Serve warm.

Parsnips are available year round in produce departments, but they are most plentiful in fall and winter. Buy small to medium-sized parsnips which are firm and well-shaped. Avoid large parsnips or any with blemishes or dried-up roots.

This recipe of parsnips and pears yields an interesting combination of flavors and textures.

PARSNIPS AND PEARS

Makes 6 servings

2 tablespoons dark brown sugar
1/8 teaspoon ground cinnamon
3 tablespoons butter or margarine, melted
4 firm, ripe pears, peeled, seeded, cut into quarters
6 medium parsnips, peeled, cut into quarters, horizontally

Cover parsnips with water and cook until just fork tender. Drain and cool.

Meanwhile, mix brown sugar and cinnamon into the melted butter.

Preheat Burton Stove Top Grill. Brush parsnips and pear pieces with melted butter. Cook parsnips and pear pieces over medium-high heat, turning once or twice. Grill until both parsnips and pear pieces are warm and tender, about 2 to 3 minutes.

Remove parsnips and pear pieces to serving dish. Serve hot.

Leeks possess a faint onion taste, although they are much milder and sweeter. Look for leeks which are well-shaped, straight and have a white base. It is the white portion of the leek which is used in cooking; the top green leaves are discarded.

Basil is a natural complement to tomatoes. Use fresh basil if possible. The smell of freshly picked basil is intense and sweet.

LEEKS WITH TOMATOES AND BASIL

Makes 4 servings

Basil butter

4 tablespoons butter or margarine, room temperature
1 tablespoon minced fresh basil

4 medium sized leeks, trimmed, washed well; leeks tend to be
    sandy
1 clove garlic, minced
1 tablespoon freshly squeezed lemon juice
2 large tomatoes, sliced
Extra virgin olive oil to brush leeks

2 tablespoons minced parsley
Salt, pepper and dried oregano to taste

Leeks With Tomatoes And Basil

Basil butter

Soften butter in a bowl, using the back of a spoon or use a food processor fitted with steel blade. Mix in basil. Remove flavored butter to a bowl. Set aside.

Cut leeks in half horizontally and brush with olive oil.

Preheat Burton Stove Top Grill. Grill leeks over medium heat, cut side down for 2 minutes. Turn leeks over and continue grilling for 1 to 2 minutes. Leeks will char slightly and be fork tender. Remove leeks to a serving dish. Sprinkle with garlic and lemon juice.

Surround leeks with sliced tomatoes. Dot leeks with basil butter. Season to taste with salt, pepper and oregano. Serve hot.

CHERRY TOMATO KABOBS WITH CHIVE BUTTER

Makes 4 servings

Chive butter

4 tablespoons butter or margarine, room temperature
2 teaspoons minced chives
1/2 teaspoon dried tarragon

16 cherry tomatoes, blossom removed
4 8-inch bamboo skewers, soaked in water 10 minutes, drained
Peanut oil for brushing grill surface

To prepare chive butter, mix softened butter with chives and tarragon using the back of a spoon or use a mini food processor. Spoon chive butter into a small bowl. Cover and set aside.

Thread tomatoes onto skewers.

Preheat Burton Stove Top Grill. Brush grill surface lightly with peanut oil. Cook skewered tomatoes over medium heat about 1 to 2 minutes, turning often. Tomatoes will begin to blister and brown, but do not let tomatoes overcook and get soggy. Remove to serving dish.

Spoon basil butter over tomatoes and serve hot.

RED ONION SLICES WITH BACON

Makes 4 servings

2 slices lean bacon, cut in half
1 large red onion
2 tablespoons minced parsley

Cut onion into thin slices, set aside.

Preheat Burton Stove Top Grill. Cook bacon strips over medium-high heat until brown and crisp, turning as needed. Drain on paper towels. Grill red onion without cleaning grill surface, 1 minute on each side. Place onions on serving dish. Crumble bacon over onion and sprinkle with parsley. Serve hot.

Shallots are milder in taste than their cousins, the onions. They tend to have a slight garlic flavor and, like garlic, the small bulbs of the shallot separate into cloves.

Hazelnuts are frequently used in dessert recipes, but their delicious flavor contributes a richness to many non-dessert foods.

LEEKS AND SHALLOTS WITH HAZELNUT BUTTER

Makes 4 servings

Hazelnut Butter

4 tablespoons butter or margarine, room temperature
2 tablespoons ground hazelnuts or peanuts
1/4 teaspoon dried tarragon

4 medium sized leeks, trimmed, washed well; leeks tend to be
    sandy
4 large shallots, sliced horizontally
1 tablespoon butter or margarine to brush shallots and leeks
1 tablespoon peanut oil
Salt and pepper to taste

Soften butter in a bowl, using the back of a spoon or use a food processor fitted with steel blade. Mix in hazelnuts and tarragon. Remove flavored butter to a bowl. Set aside.

Leeks And Shallots With Hazelnut Butter

Cut leeks in half horizontally. Slice shallots thinly.

Preheat Burton Stove Top Grill. Brush leeks with melted butter. Grill leeks over medium-high heat, cut side down for 2 minutes.

Turn leeks over and continue grilling for 1 to 2 minutes. Leeks will char slightly and be fork tender. Remove leeks to serving dish. Dot with flavored butter.

Grill shallots, quickly for about 1 minute per side. Brush shallots with butter as they cook, turning frequently until shallots soften. Sprinkle shallots over leeks.

Dot with hazelnut butter and serve hot.

Fennel is native to southern Europe, but now is commonly cultivated in the U.S. This vegetable has a mild licorice flavor; in fact, the oil of fennel makes up ninety percent of the essential oil in anise. Fennel makes a wonderful accompaniment with fish and with pork. The freshest bulbs of fennel are well-rounded and are pale green to white. Deep green bulbs are over-ripe.

FENNEL

Makes 4 servings

1 tablespoon caraway seeds
2 tablespoons butter or margarine, melted
2 tablespoons freshly squeezed lemon juice
4 tablespoons freshly grated Parmesan cheese
4 fennel bulbs

Trim and slice fennel bulbs into 1/2 to 1/4 inch slices. Cover fennel with salted water in saucepan. Bring to a boil over medium heat. Reduce heat to simmer. Continue cooking uncovered until fennel slices are fork tender, about 6 to 8 minutes. Drain, cool.

Mix caraway seeds into butter and brush fennel slices.

Fennel

Preheat Burton Stove Top Grill. Cook fennel slices over medium-high heat for about 1 minute on each side. Fennel will brown slightly on the outside and be tender on the inside.

Remove fennel slices to serving dish. Sprinkle with freshly grated Parmesan cheese and serve hot.

Green tomatoes are unripened, but they are excellent when grilled. Pick and use these immature tomatoes in early spring or in the fall.

The following recipe is a good use for the fall bounty.

GREEN TOMATOES

Makes 4 servings

3/4 cup cornmeal
1/4 teaspoon each ingredient: garlic powder, dried sage
Salt and pepper to taste
3 large green tomatoes, cut into 1/2 inch slices

Peanut oil for brushing grill surface
2 tablespoons minced parsley

Mix cornmeal with garlic, sage, salt and pepper. Spread on a flat plate. Dust both sides of green tomato slices with flavored cornmeal.

Preheat Burton Stove Top Grill. Brush grill surface lightly with oil. Cook tomato slices over medium-high heat about 1 to 2 minutes per side. Turn tomatoes once during grilling. Tomatoes will be crusty on the outside and warm on the inside.

Remove tomato slices to serving plate; sprinkle with minced parsley. Serve tomato slices hot.

Red bell peppers are not hot, but have a mild sweet taste. While this recipe calls for red peppers, you may use green or yellow bell peppers with equal success. Bell peppers may be stored in the refrigerator, but they will not hold their freshness and texture over a few days. Choose bright-colored, firm and well-shaped bell peppers.

RED PEPPER STRIPS
WITH TOMATO CONCASSE

Makes 4 servings

Tomato Concasse (recipe follows)

4 large red bell peppers

Preheat Burton Stove Top Grill. Cook peppers over high heat until charred on all sides. Using a fork, transfer the peppers to a plastic bag. Close the bag and let the peppers stand for 20 minutes. Remove peppers from the bag. Peel off the skin; discard the stems and seeds.

Slice the peppers into thin strips. Arrange peppers decoratively on a plate. Top with tomato concasse.

Tomato Concasse

2 pounds ripe tomatoes
1/2 teaspoon each ingredient: salt, dried basil
1/4 teaspoon pepper

Red Pepper Strips With Tomato Concasse

Peel, seed and roughly chop the tomatoes. Put tomatoes in colander or sieve, and let drain 5 minutes. Remove tomatoes to serving dish. Sprinkle tomatoes with salt and basil. Cover and refrigerate until needed. Stir before serving.

It has been said that "eating an artichoke is like getting to know someone really well". The edible parts of the leaves of the artichoke are the fleshy bases.

ARTICHOKE AND MUSHROOM KABOBS

Makes 4 servings

Lemon Marinade

1/2 freshly squeezed lemon or lime
4 tablespoons extra virgin olive oil
1 tablespoon dried basil
1/2 teaspoon garlic powder
2 bay leaves

1 can, 14 1/2 ounces, artichoke hearts, drained
12 medium mushrooms, cleaned and trimmed
4 bamboo skewers, soaked in water 10 minutes, drained

To prepare marinade, combine juice, oil, basil, garlic and bay leaves. Pour marinade into self-sealing plastic bag. Add artichokes and mushrooms. Seal bag securely closed. Turn bag several times so that the marinade will coat all the vegetables. Refrigerate and marinate for 2 hours. Drain, discard marinade.

Artichoke and Mushroom Kabobs

Thread artichokes and mushrooms alternately onto skewers.

Preheat Burton Stove Top Grill. Grill vegetable kabobs over medium heat for 3 to 4 minutes, turning every minute, or as necessary. Cook until vegetables are tender or to taste. Vegetables will begin to brown on the outside and be tender on the inside. Remove kabobs from the grill, set decoratively on the platter and serve on buffet or pass at the table. Serve hot or room temperature.

Plantains are available in Hispanic markets. They are similar in shape and size to a banana, but not sweet. The plantains must be cooked before eating.

PLANTAINS

Makes 4 to 6 servings

Salt to taste
3 tablespoons minced cilantro, divided
2 tablespoons butter or margarine, melted
3 large, ripe plantains, available at Hispanic food stores

Peel and cut plantains in 1/2 inch pieces. Press down on plantain slices with a spatula. Put plantain slices on a dish, set aside.

Mix 1/2 tablespoon of cilantro with the melted butter. Brush plantain slices with flavored margarine.

Preheat Burton Stove Top Grill. Cook plantain slices over medium heat about 1 minute on each side. Plantains will be a golden brown on the outside and tender and warm on the inside. Remove plantain slices to serving dish.

Sprinkle with salt and remaining cilantro. Serve hot. Good as an appetizer or a vegetable course.

ACORN SQUASH WITH BROWN SUGAR

Makes 4 servings

2 acorn squash, cut in half, seeded
2 tablespoons butter or margarine, melted
1/4 cup firmly packed dark brown sugar
1/4 teaspoon each ingredient: salt, pepper, ground cinnamon
1/2 cup chopped walnuts

Cover acorn squash halves with cold water in a large saucepan. Bring to a boil over medium heat and continue cooking for 20 minutes or until the squash are just fork tender, yet firm. Drain and cool. Peel squash.

Peel and cut squash into 1/2 inch rings. Mix melted butter with sugar, salt, pepper and ground cinnamon. Brush squash rings with flavored butter.

Preheat Burton Stove Top Grill. Grill squash rings over medium heat for 1 minute on each side. Squash will begin to brown on each side. Place squash on serving plate and sprinkle with walnuts. Serve hot.

ZUCCHINI TWO WAYS
WITH ALMONDS OR TOMATO SAUCE

Makes 4 servings

1/4 teaspoon each ingredient: garlic powder, salt, pepper
Extra virgin olive oil for brushing zucchini
3 small zucchini, approximately 4 inches long, cut into half,
**   horizontally**
1/2 cup slivered almonds

Mix garlic powder, salt and pepper into olive oil. Brush zucchini with flavored oil.

Preheat Burton Stove Top Grill. Cook zucchini, cut side down, over medium heat for 1 1/2 minutes. Brush zucchini again with flavored oil and turn zucchini over. Grill for 1 to 2 minutes or until zucchini are cooked to taste. Zucchini will be fork tender. Remove zucchini to serving plate. Sprinkle with slivered almonds.

Zucchini With Tomato Sauce

Tomato Sauce

2 tablespoons extra virgin olive oil
2 cloves garlic, minced
1 onion, minced
1/2 pound ground beef
1 can, 28 ounces, tomatoes, undrained
1 can, 6 ounces, tomato paste
2 bay leaves
3/4 teaspoon dried basil
1/2 teaspoon each ingredient: dried oregano, salt
1/4 teaspoon freshly ground pepper

Heat olive oil in frying pan over medium heat. Sauté garlic and onion for 4 minutes, stirring occasionally. Mix in ground beef and cook until the meat is just browned, about 10 minutes. Add tomatoes and juice, tomato paste, bay leaves, basil, oregano, salt and pepper. Simmer uncovered until sauce thickens, 45 minutes, stirring occasionally. Discard bay leaves. To serve, place grilled zucchini on serving dish and cover with tomato sauce. Serve hot.

Chanterelles are dainty, trumpet-shaped, reddish golden mushrooms which can be found wild in deciduous woods. Warning: never eat or cook with a wild mushroom that has not been positively identified. Chanterelles have a slight apricot taste. Regular button mushrooms may be substituted for chanterelles.

The chanterelle mushroom is a wild mushroom that has a somewhat nutty, yet delicate taste. They are available in large supermarkets.

CHANTERELLE MUSHROOMS

Makes 4 servings

1 pound Chanterelle mushrooms
2 tablespoons butter or margarine, melted
1 tablespoon peanut oil
1/4 teaspoon each ingredient: dried tarragon, pepper
1/4 cup minced parsley

Trim, wash and pat dry chanterelle mushrooms with paper towels.

Mix melted butter and peanut oil together with dried tarragon and pepper. Brush mushrooms with flavored butter.

Preheat Burton Stove Top Grill. Cook mushrooms over medium heat, in a single layer, for about 2 to 3 minutes. Turn mushrooms as needed. Mushrooms should be warm and a golden brown. Remove to serving dish. Serve mushrooms hot.

Polenta is prepared with yellow corn meal and is served as a main dish or as a vegetable. I prepare polenta in the classical style and then grill it.

POLENTA WITH TOMATO SAUCE

Makes 4 to 6 servings

4 cups water
2 teaspoons salt
1 1/2 cups yellow cornmeal
2 tablespoons butter or margarine

Tomato Sauce

4 large tomatoes, chopped
1/2 cup chopped celery
1 red bell pepper, seeded, chopped
1/2 teaspoon each ingredient: dried basil, salt
1/2 teaspoon prepared mustard
1/4 cup sugar
1/4 cup cider vinegar

Grease loaf pan with olive oil.

Bring salted water to a boil over high heat. Add cornmeal in a slow steady stream, stirring constantly with a wooden spoon pressing out lumps. Stir until all the cornmeal has been added. Simmer and stir continuously for 45 minutes. Mixture will be thick and pull away from sides of pan. Mix in butter.

Polenta With Tomato Sauce

Pour polenta into prepared pan. Cool and refrigerate polenta, about 1 hour. Remove polenta from pan, cut into 1/2 inch slices.

While polenta is in refrigerator, prepare tomato sauce. Combine tomatoes, celery and pepper in a deep bowl. In a small separate bowl, combine basil, salt, mustard, sugar and vinegar. Toss to combine ingredients. Cover and refrigerate until needed. Taste to adjust seasonings, and toss before serving.

Preheat Burton Stove Top Grill. Brush 6 polenta slices with oil. Cook polenta over medium-high heat for 2 minutes per side. Polenta will brown slightly on the outside and be warm on the inside. Serve polenta hot with tomato sauce.

POLENTA WITH SAGE

Makes 4 servings

4 cups water
2 teaspoons salt
1 1/2 cups yellow cornmeal
1/2 teaspoon dried sage or 1 teaspoon fresh sage
2 tablespoons butter or margarine, melted
2 tablespoons extra virgin olive oil
1/2 teaspoon dried sage

Grease loaf pan.

Bring salted water to a boil over high heat. Add cornmeal in a slow steady stream, stirring constantly with a wooden spoon pressing out lumps. Stir until all the cornmeal has been added. Stir in sage and cook for 45 minutes; continue stirring often, over low heat. Mixture will be thick and pull away from the sides of the pan. Mix in butter.

Pour polenta into prepared pan. Cool and refrigerate until set, about 1 hour. Remove polenta from pan. Cut polenta into 1/2 inch slices. Blend olive oil and sage together.

Preheat Burton Stove Top Grill. Brush polenta slices with oil mixture. Cook polenta over medium-high heat for 2 minutes per side or until polenta is just browned on the outside and warm on the inside. Serve hot.

Always use fresh garlic. Too often cooks use garlic which has been allowed to turn brown, the sign that the garlic will be stale and rancid. To ensure that garlic will be fresh, buy in small quantities and buy frequently. Store garlic in a cool, dry, dark place.

GARLIC POTATOES

Makes 4 servings

4 large potatoes, peeled
4 tablespoons butter or margarine, melted
1/2 teaspoon each ingredient: garlic powder, dried oregano, salt

Bring salted water to a boil over high heat; add potatoes. Cook over medium heat until potatoes are just fork tender. Drain and cool. Slice each potato horizontally into 6 wedges.

Mix melted butter with garlic powder and oregano. Brush potatoes with flavored butter.

Preheat Burton Stove Top Grill. Cook potatoes over medium-high heat, about 3 minutes. Turn potatoes so that all sides will brown slightly.

Remove potatoes to serving dish. Serve hot.

SWEET POTATO CHIPS

Makes 4 servings

3 large sweet potatoes
3 tablespoons butter or margarine, melted
1 tablespoon peanut oil
1/2 teaspoon garlic powder
1/4 teaspoon ground nutmeg
Salt

Peel the sweet potatoes. Cut in half. Cover potatoes with salted water in a large saucepan. Bring to a boil, reduce heat and cook over medium heat for 15 to 20 minutes or until potatoes are fork tender but still firm. Drain potatoes and cool.

Slice potatoes 1/4 to 1/2 inch thick slices and set on a plate. Mix melted butter with garlic powder and ground nutmeg. Brush potatoes with flavored butter.

Preheat Burton Stove Top Grill. Cook sweet potato slices over medium-high heat for about 1 minute per side or until potatoes are cooked and warm on the inside and crisp on the outside. Remove to serving dish; sprinkle with salt. Serve hot.

Oregano is widely used in Italian dishes, particularly those with tomato and cheese. Dried oregano imparts a strong and pungent flavor to this potato dish.

Parsley makes a fine window-box or potted vegetable. It can be grown year round and used for flavoring or as a garnish with a wide variety of dishes.

POTATOES ITALIAN

Makes 4 servings

1 pound small, red new potatoes
2 tablespoons extra virgin olive oil
2 cloves garlic, minced
1 teaspoon dried oregano
1 1/2 tablespoons minced parsley
3 tomatoes, chopped
Salt and pepper to taste

2 tablespoons butter or margarine, melted
2 tablespoons peanut oil

Cover potatoes with salted water in a large pan. Bring to a boil, reduce heat to medium and continue cooking until potatoes are done but still firm. Cool. Peel and slice potatoes into 1/4 inch thick slices.

While potatoes are cooking, heat oil in a frying pan. Sauté for 1 minute. Stir in oregano, parsley and tomatoes. Season with salt and pepper to taste. Simmer for 5 to 6 minutes, stirring occasionally. Remove from heat.

Potatoes Italian

Mix butter and peanut oil together. Preheat Burton Stove Top Grill. Brush potato slices with oil mixture; cook over medium-high heat until crispy on the outside and warm on the inside, about 1 to 2 minutes. Turn potatoes once during grilling; brush with oil as you turn. Remove potatoes to serving bowl.

RED CABBAGE WITH GRILLED APPLE RINGS

Makes 4 servings

4 tablespoons butter or margarine
1 medium head red cabbage, shredded
2 Granny Smith apples, peeled, cored, chopped
1/2 teaspoon salt
1/4 teaspoon each ingredient: pepper, nutmeg
5 tablespoons white vinegar
5 tablespoons dark brown sugar
1/2 cup dark raisins

Grilled Apple Rings

2 tablespoons butter or margarine, melted
1 tablespoon peanut oil
1/2 teaspoon grated lemon zest
2 large Granny Smith apples, peeled, cored, cut in 1/4 inch
    rings

Heat butter in a large heavy saucepan. Add cabbage and apples. Sprinkle cabbage with salt, nutmeg, pepper, vinegar and sugar. Cook over medium heat, stirring occasionally for 35 minutes, covered. Check cabbage after 10 minutes. If it is too dry, add 1/2 cup water or as needed.

When ready to serve, preheat Burton Stove Top Grill. Mix butter, oil and zest together. Brush apple slices with butter mixture. Cook apple rings over medium-high grill for 1 minute on each side. Apples will be a golden brown on the outside and still firm on the inside.

Red Cabbage With Grilled Apple Rings

Spoon hot cooked cabbage into serving dish. Arrange apple rings decoratively over top. Serve hot.

DESSERTS

Desserts go well with the Burton Stove Top Grill and the results, warm from the grill, will be both rewarding and heart-warming, the perfect conclusion for many meals.

Fruit works very well on the Burton grill, and you can obtain many delectable combinations of warm, grilled fruits and cheeses. Liqueur flavorings and sauces may be used with most grilled fruits. One of my all-time favorite desserts is grilled pineapple slices, either served alone or covered with warm cheese.

One of the best dessert tastes of all is that of grilled fresh pineapple.

PINEAPPLE SLICES OVER PINEAPPLE SHERBET

Makes 4 servings

4 scoops pineapple sherbet

1 tablespoon honey
3 tablespoons butter or margarine, melted

1 fresh pineapple, crown discarded, peeled

Combine honey and melted butter in a small bowl.

Slice pineapple into 1/2 inch, mound slices.

Preheat Burton Stove Top Grill over medium-high heat. Brush pineapple slices with honey mixture. Grill pineapple about 1 1/2 minutes per side.

Quickly arrange pineapple slices on dessert dishes. Place a scoop of pineapple sherbet in the center of the dish. Serve at once. Good with cookies.

Fruit kabobs are an often over-looked grill dish that can be used as a sweet salad or as a dessert.

FRUIT KABOBS WITH WARM POUND CAKE

Makes 6 servings

Raspberry Sauce

1 package, 10 ounces, raspberries, defrosted, juice included
2 teaspoons freshly squeezed lime juice
1/4 cup sugar

6 8-inch long bamboo skewers, soaked in water 10 minutes,
     drained
1 can, 5 1/2 ounces, pineapple chunks, drained
2 bananas, cut into 1 inch pieces
3 1-inch thick slices pound cake, cut in 1 inch cubes

4 tablespoons melted margarine or butter
1 tablespoon dark rum, optional

To prepare sauce, purée raspberries in a food processor fitted with steel blade. Combine juice and sugar with raspberries in a small saucepan. Simmer for 3 to 4 minutes. Strain sauce, discarding seeds. Set aside.

Thread skewers, with pineapple chunks, bananas and pound cake.

Mix butter and rum together.

Brush kabobs with butter mixture.

Fruit Kabobs With Warm Pound Cake

Preheat Burton Stove Top Grill. Cook kabobs over medium-high heat, just until hot. Do not let them melt. Turn kabobs often, brushing as you turn. Remove from grill.

Spoon raspberry sauce into individual dishes. Set kabobs on each plate over the sauce. Serve immediately.

STRAWBERRIES OVER
STRAWBERRY ICE CREAM

Makes 4 servings

4 double scoops strawberry ice cream

Hot Fudge Sauce

3/4 cup good quality cocoa
1 cup sugar
1 cup evaporated milk
1/2 cup light corn syrup
1/2 cup butter or margarine
1 1/2 teaspoons vanilla

20 large, firm strawberries, washed

4 bamboo skewers, soaked in water 10 minutes, drained

To make hot fudge sauce, mix cocoa and sugar in a saucepan. Mix in milk and corn syrup. Simmer, stirring often until sauce comes to a boil. Continue cooking, stirring constantly, for 30 seconds. Remove syrup from heat. Whisk in butter and vanilla. Remove from heat. Serve sauce warm.

Strawberries Over Strawberry Ice Cream

Drain strawberries on paper towels. Leave hulls intact. Thread strawberries on skewers. Preheat Burton Stove Top Grill. Cook berries over medium heat, just to warm them. Do not let berries get mushy. Cook about 30 seconds on each side.

To serve, put one double scoop of strawberry ice cream into sauce dishes. Ladle hot fudge sauce over ice cream. Set warm strawberries over top of the ice cream. Serve immediately.

ORANGE SLICES WITH BLUEBERRIES

Makes 4 servings

4 large navel oranges, peeled, cut into 1/4 inch slices
1 cup dry sherry, divided
1 pint blueberries
2 tablespoons dry sherry
3 tablespoons light brown sugar
2 tablespoons butter or margarine

Place orange slices in a bowl. Sprinkle sherry over the oranges. Let stand at room temperature for 1 hour, turning once. Drain.

Meanwhile pick over blueberries, discarding any bruised berries. Wash berries and drain on paper towels.

Toss berries with sherry. Set aside.

Preheat Burton Stove Top Grill. Mix sugar and butter together. Brush grill surface with butter. Grill orange slices over medium heat, 1 minute on each side. Set warm orange slices on dessert dishes. Sprinkle with blueberries and serve immediately.

Golden brown, grilled papaya slices are wonderful fresh from the grill. Again, the blueberries give a pleasing color combination to this dessert.

PAPAYA WITH BLUEBERRIES

Makes 4 servings

2 cups low-fat vanilla yogurt
1/3 cup firmly packed light brown sugar
3 tablespoons dark rum

1 papaya (enough for 4 servings)
4 tablespoons butter or margarine
1 pint fresh or defrosted blueberries

Mix the yogurt, sugar and rum together. Spoon into a bowl. Refrigerate until serving time.

Peel, seed and cut the papaya into 3/4 inch spears. Brush papaya with butter. Preheat Burton Stove Top Grill. Cook papaya over medium heat, about 1 to 1 1/2 minutes on each side. Remove to serving dish. Serve immediately sprinkled with blueberries and vanilla yogurt.

Brie is truly one of the world's greatest, most exquisite cheeses. It is a natural warming, oozing, soft perfection on the grill.

FRUIT SALAD WITH GRILLED BRIE CHEESE

Makes 4 servings

1 medium cantaloupe, peeled
1/2 honeydew, peeled
4 lettuce leaves
2 cups watermelon cubes
1/2 pound seedless green or red grapes, cut in small bunches
4 ounces brie cheese
1 cup lemon yogurt
1/2 cup slivered almonds

Cut cantaloupe and honeydew into wedges, discard seeds.

Arrange lettuce leaves on each plate. Divide and arrange cantaloupe and honeydew decoratively on lettuce. Place watermelon and grapes around lettuce.

Cut brie cheese into 4 portions. Preheat Burton Stove Top Grill. Cook brie over medium heat for about 30 seconds on each side. Brie should be just warm and about to be runny.

Remove cheese from grill and set on fruit plates. Spoon a dollop of lemon yogurt in the center of the fruit plates and sprinkle with almonds. Eat at once.

S'Mores are one of the great delights of childhood. Adults can't turn them down easily, for that matter.

S'MORES

Makes 4 servings

3 chocolate bars, 5 ounces each
8 large marshmallows, or to taste
8 squares graham crackers

Set half of a chocolate bar on 1 graham cracker. Place 2 large marshmallows in center over chocolate. Press remaining graham cracker into place, forming the famous graham cracker sandwich called s'mores. Wrap each s'more in aluminum foil.

Preheat Burton Stove Top Grill. Cook s'mores over medium-high heat for 1 minute on each side. Serve immediately.

Bananas Foster was created and popularized at Brennan's Restaurant in New Orleans during the 1950's. Today it is a rich and favorite dessert throughout the country.

BANANAS FOSTER

Makes 4 servings

4 double scoops vanilla ice cream
3 tablespoons butter or margarine, melted
1 teaspoon peanut oil
3 tablespoons light brown sugar
1/4 teaspoon ground cinnamon
1/8 teaspoon ground nutmeg
4 large firm bananas, cut in half horizontally

Mix melted butter with peanut oil, brown sugar, cinnamon and nutmeg. Brush bananas with flavored butter mixture.

Preheat Burton Stove Top Grill. Cook bananas over medium-high heat for 1 minute on each side. Set ice cream in 4 sauce dishes. Quickly set bananas over ice cream. Serve immediately.

PEACHES WITH BOURBON SAUCE

Makes 4 servings

Bourbon Sauce

1 cup heavy cream or half and half
1/4 cup sugar
4 egg yolks
1/8 teaspoon ground nutmeg
1/4 cup bourbon
4 ripe peaches
Butter or margarine to brush peaches

Mix cream and sugar together in a small saucepan. Simmer, stirring continuously until the sugar has melted. Remove mixture from heat and cool.

Beat egg yolks with nutmeg until light. In a slow steady stream, add cream mixture, beating as you incorporate ingredients.

Pour sauce in the top pan of a double boiler over simmering water. Simmer for 5 minutes, stirring often. Mixture will thicken slightly.

Pour sauce into a bowl, stir in bourbon, cover and chill until ready to serve.

Blanch peaches, slip off skin. Cut peaches in half, discard stone. Brush with butter.

Peaches With Bourbon Sauce

Preheat Burton Stove Top Grill. Cook peaches over medium heat, cut side down for 2 minutes. Turn over and grill for 1 minute over medium-high heat. Remove peaches to individual serving dishes. Pass bourbon sauce at table, allowing guests to help themselves. Good with cookies.

This is a very interesting combination of tastes. The coffee sauce is a mixture of yogurt and coffee liqueur.

PEARS WITH COFFEE LIQUEUR SAUCE

Makes 4 servings

Coffee Liqueur Sauce

1 cup small curd cottage cheese
1 cup non-dairy whipped cream
1/2 cup light brown sugar
1 cup vanilla yogurt
1/3 cup coffee flavored liqueur
1/2 teaspoon ground cinnamon

2 tablespoons butter or margarine, melted
1 teaspoon peanut oil
1/4 teaspoon ground cinnamon
2 tablespoons sugar
4 ripe pears, quartered, cored

To make the sauce, purée cottage cheese in food processor fitted with steel blade. Remove cheese and place in a bowl. Blend in whipped cream, sugar, yogurt and coffee flavored liqueur and cinnamon. Cover and refrigerate until ready to serve. Can be prepared day before serving.

Mix butter with peanut oil, cinnamon and sugar. Brush pears with butter mixture.

Pears With Coffee Liqueur Sauce

Preheat Burton Stove Top Grill. Cook pear quarters over medium-high heat for 1 minute on each side. Remove pear pieces, divide evenly, and place into 4 sauce dishes. Top with coffee liqueur sauce. Pass extra sauce at table. Good served with coffee and small cookies.

CHESTNUTS

Makes 4 servings

4 8-inch bamboo skewers, soaked in water 10 minutes, drained
2 cups heavy cream, whipped
3 tablespoons butter or margarine, melted
1 teaspoon orange zest
1 jar, 8 ounces, whole chestnuts, drained
1 1/2 teaspoons vanilla
1/2 cup sugar

Thread chestnuts onto bamboo skewers. Mix melted butter with orange zest. Brush chestnuts with flavored butter. Set aside.

Spoon whipped cream into a bowl. Mix with vanilla and sugar. Divide the cream into dessert dishes.

Preheat Burton Stove Top Grill. Cook chestnuts over medium-high heat until warm, about 2 to 3 minutes, turning after each minute. Set a chestnut skewer over whipped cream. Enjoy.

Honeydew melons are incredibly sweet and juicy. The pale green color of the honeydew slices makes an elegant and lovely dessert when paired with the rich red of the strawberries.

HONEYDEW WEDGES WITH BERRIES

Makes 4 servings

1 small ripe honeydew
3 tablespoons butter or margarine, melted
2 tablespoons Grand Marnier Liqueur
1 teaspoon orange zest

2 cups strawberries

Cut honeydew in half, discard seeds. Peel off skin using a paring knife. Cut melon into 3/4 inch wedges. Arrange melon on a plate.

Mix melted butter with Grand Marnier and orange zest. Brush honeydew wedges with flavored butter.

Wash, hull the strawberries. Pat dry with paper towels and slice. Refrigerate strawberries until ready to serve.

Preheat Burton Stove Top Grill. Cook honeydew wedges over medium heat for 1 minute on each side. Remove to a serving dish. Scatter strawberries over warm melon wedges. Sprinkle with mint leaves, if available. Serve immediately.

This dessert is richer than most due to the use of Sabayon sauce which is traditionally a blending of egg yolks, wine and sugar. In this recipe, however, I have used cider in place of wine.

APPLE ROUNDS WITH CIDER SABAYON SAUCE

Makes 4 servings

4 ripe apples, such as Golden Delicious
2 tablespoons freshly squeezed lemon juice
1 cup sugar
1/2 teaspoon ground cinnamon
Melted butter or margarine to brush grill surface

Cider Sabayon Sauce

6 egg yolks
1/2 cup sugar
1/4 cup brandy
3/4 cup apple cider

Peel and core apples. Cut them in 1/2 inch rounds. Place apple slices in a bowl. Sprinkle with lemon juice. Mix sugar and cinnamon together and spread on a plate. Roll apple slices in sugar.

Preheat Burton Stove Top Grill. Brush grill surface with butter. Cook apple slices over medium heat for 1 minute on each side. Place apple slices on separate dessert dishes. Prepare sabayon sauce.

Apple Rounds With Cider Sabayon Sauce

Just before serving, bring water to a boil in the bottom half of a double boiler over medium heat. Whisk together egg yolks, sugar, brandy and cider in top half of double boiler. Reduce heat to simmer and set the top half of pan over the simmering water. Whisk the cider mixture until it is foamy and has doubled in volume.

Spoon cider sabayon sauce over apples. Serve immediately.

INDEX

Warmed Corned Beef on Rye, 97
Whitefish with Grilled Green
    Onions, 226
Wild Rice Salad, 154
Whole Wheat Hamburger Rolls
    with Poppy Seeds, 28

Yogurt Cucumber Dressing, 51
Yogurt Marinade, 174

Zucchini Two Ways with Almonds
    or Tomato Sauce, 265